PASS THRU FIRE

Lou Reed

PASS THRU FIRE

The Collected Lyrics

BLOOMSBURY

ALBUM COVER CREDITS

Time Rocker Robert Wilson, 1996
Legendary Hearts, Mistrial, New Sensations, Metal Machine Music, Sally Can't Dance, Lou Reed, Berlin, Transformer, Coney Island Baby
Used Courtesy of The RCA Records Label
VU, 1969 Velvet Underground Live, Another View
Courtesy of Universal Music Group
The Velvet Underground & Nico, The Velvet Underground, White Light/White Heat
Courtesy of PolyGram Records, Inc.
Street Hassle, Rock and Roll Heart, Growing Up in Public, The Bells, The Blue Mask
Courtesy of Arista Records, Inc.

Loaded Courtesy of Rhino
Songs for Drella 1990 Sire Records Company for the US
New York 1989 Sire Records Company for the US and WEA International Inc. for the world outside the US

Magic and Loss Used Courtesy of Louis Jammes
The Velvet Underground Live MCMXCIII © ℗ 1993 Sire Records Company for the US and WEA International Inc. for the world outside of the US

Book design by Sagmeister Inc.

First published in Great Britain 2000
This paperback edition published 2002
The moral right of the author has been asserted
Bloomsbury Publishing Plc, 38 Soho Square, London W1D 3HB
A CIP record for this book is available from the British Library
ISBN 0 7475 5893 0
10 9 8 7 6 5 4 3 2 1
Printed in Great Britain by St Edmundsbury Press, Suffolk

For L.A.

Bob Miller for signing us, Leigh Haber for her encouragement, Andrew Wylie for making it happen, Stefan Sagmeister for his enduring brilliance and fun, Karin Greenfield-Sanders, Beth Groubert, Roger Moenks and Mike Rathke for the meat and potatoes hard stuff.

Pass thru Fire

The exact line is " . . . Pass thru Fire licking at your lips. . . ." My other favorite line is " . . . there's a door up ahead not a wall." There are many favorite lines of mine that run through the album "Magic and Loss." It was originally intended to be about Magic, real magic, the ability to make oneself disappear. I had heard stories of magicians in Mexico with strange powers. I thought if I put out songs about magic they would get in touch with me and tell me their secrets. After all, people are always telling me their secrets, and I often put them in song as though they happened to me. Unfortunately two friends died of a virulent cancer within one year of each other while I was writing and so "Magic" became "Magic and Loss." I wished for a magical way to deal with grief and disappearance. I wanted to create a music that helped with loss. It seemed we are always starting over, given a chance to deal with things again.

In the "New York" album I'm struck again by the interest in outside forces. "Caught between the twisted stars. . . ." The stars are twisted, the map is faulty. Romeo Rodriguez loses his soul in someone's rented car. A bleak environment to start out in. But predictable enough if you believe the dictum of one of my earliest songs, "I'll Be Your Mirror," where the singer offers to ". . . reflect what you are, in case you don't know." That was a love song, but the ability and desire to reflect can go other places, and show us other rooms and conditions within and about us.

I have always thought my lyrics went beyond reportage and took emotional albeit nonmoral stances. In the early lyrics this was often seen as a celebration or glorification of what was commonly seen as sin. Sinful behavior and actions going unpunished. That this occurred in a recording was of itself thought sinful. A recorded cauldron of sin. This plus the backing of Andy Warhol made for an incendiary brew. I came back to these times in "Songs for Drella," which was an attempt to give you a feeling for the times and the man and the position of respect he held in our eyes as an artist. It's wonderful to this day to see how he manipulated and handled the press, his extreme work ethic, his attempts to stay relevant in a world geared to the latest whatever. The new generation looks to define itself and the first thing it does is throw away the prior, the old.

In *Time Rocker*, a play that I did with Robert Wilson, we were interested in transcending time, passing through it and its various boundaries and worlds. This type of travel meant something to me being a form of magic. We didn't have a rented car but a time traveling fish. It brings me back to the desire in "Trade In" from "Set the Twilight Reeling" to transcend oneself to trade your very soul the very same soul that was " . . . up for grabs . . . " in "Coney Island Baby." The same Average Guy in "The Blue Mask" who put " . . . pins through the nipples in his chest and thought he was a saint." Love and the desire for transcendence run through these songs. "The Proposition"; "Make Up My Mind"; "Wild Side" for that matter. The characters in these songs are always moving toward something, there is conflict and they try to deal with it. In "Some Kind of Love" he " . . . put(s) jelly on your shoulder." While later trying to "Hang on to Your Emotion" so that you can "Set the Twilight Reeling" as the ". . . moon and stars sit set before my window." The actresses relate because they're acting. They understand the desire to see "The Bells," to hear the announcement of transcendence and freedom. And that's what all the lyrics are about.

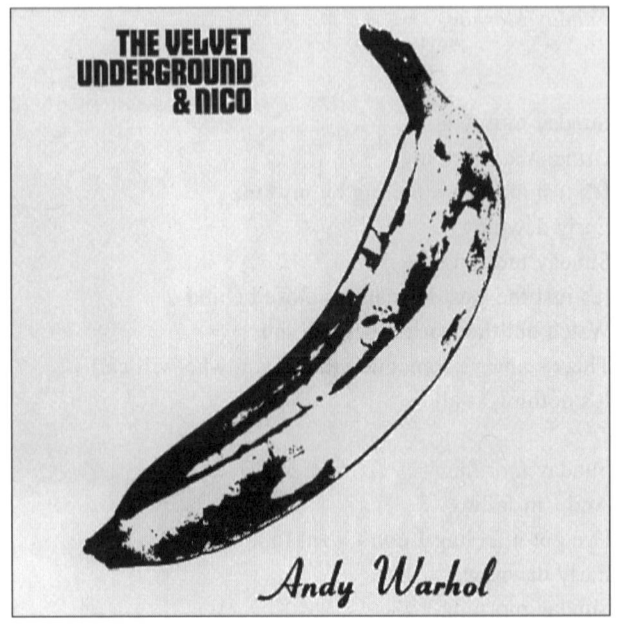
THE VELVET
UNDERGROUND
& NICO
Andy Warhol

Sunday Morning

Sunday morning
Brings the dawn in
It's just a restless feeling by my side
Early dawning
Sunday morning
It's just the wasted years so close behind
Watch out the world's behind you
There's always someone around you who will call
It's nothing at all

Sunday morning
And I'm falling
I've got a feeling I don't want to know
Early dawning
Sunday morning
It's all the streets you crossed not so long ago
Watch out the world's behind you
There's always someone around you who will call
It's nothing at all

Sunday morning

I'm Waiting for the Man

I'm waiting for my man
Twentysix dollars in my hand
Up to Lexington 1-2-5
Feeling sick and dirty more dead than alive
I'm waiting for my man

Hey white boy, what you doin' uptown
Hey white boy, you chasin' our women around
Oh pardon me sir, it's furthest from my mind
I'm just lookin' for a dear dear friend of mine
I'm waiting for my man

Here he comes, he's all dressed in black
PR shoes and a big straw hat
He's never early, he's always late
First thing you learn is that you always gotta to wait
I'm waiting for my man
Up to a brownstone, up three flights of stairs
Everybody's pinned you but nobody cares
He's got the works gives you sweet taste
Then you gotta split because you got no time to waste
I'm waiting for my man

Baby don't you holler, darlin' don't you ball and shout
I'm feeling good, you know I'm gonna work it on out
I'm feeling good, I'm feeling oh so fine
Until tomorrow but that's just some other time
I'm waiting for my man

Femme Fatale

Here she comes
You'd better watch your step
She's going to break your heart in two, it's true
It's not hard to realize
Just look into her false-colored eyes
She'll build you up to just put you down
What a clown

'Cause everybody knows
The things she does to please
She's just a little tease
See the way she walks
Hear the way she talks

You're written in her book
You're number 37, have a look
She's going to smile to make you frown, what a clown
Little boy, she's from the street
Before you start you're already beat
She's going to play you for a fool, yes it's true

'Cause everybody knows
The things she does to please
She's just a little tease
See the way she walks
Hear the way she talks

She's a femme fatale

Venus in Furs

Shiny shiny, shiny boots of leather
Whiplash girlchild in the dark
Comes in bells, your servant, don't forsake him
Strike dear mistress and cure his heart

Downy sins of streetlight fancies
Chase the costumes she shall wear
Ermine furs adorn imperious
Severin Severin awaits you there

I am tired, I am weary
I could sleep for a thousand years
A thousand dreams that would awake me
Different colors made of tears

Kiss the boot of shiny shiny leather
Shiny leather in the dark
Tongue the thongs, the belt that does await you
Strike dear mistress and cure his heart

Severin, Severin, speak so slightly
Severin, down on your bended knee
Taste the whip, in love not given lightly
Taste the whip, now bleed for me

Shiny shiny, shiny boots of leather
Whiplash girlchild in the dark
Severin your servant, comes in bells, please don't forsake him
Strike dear mistress and cure his heart

Run Run Run

Teenage Mary said to Uncle Dave
I sold my soul, must be saved
Gonna take a walk down Union Square
You never know who you gonna find there

You gotta run run run run run
Gypsy death and you
Tell you what to do

Margarita Passion I had to get her fixed
She wasn't well, she's getting sick
Went to sell her soul, she wasn't high
Didn't know things she could buy

Seasick Sarah had a golden nose
Hard-nailed boots, wrapped around her toes
When she turned blue, all the angels screamed
They didn't know, they couldn't make the scene

Beardless Harry, what a waste
Couldn't even get a small-town taste
Rode the trolleys, down to Forty-Seven
Figured if he was good, he'd get himself to heaven

We gotta run run run run run
Take a drag or two
Run run run run run
Gypsy death and you
Tell you what to do

All Tomorrow's Parties

And what costume shall the poor girl wear
To all tomorrow's parties
A hand-me-down dress from who knows where
To all tomorrow's parties
And where will she go, and what shall she do
When midnight comes around
She'll turn once more to Sunday's clown and cry behind the door

And what costume shall the poor girl wear
To all tomorrow's parties
Why silks and linens of yesterday's gowns
To all tomorrow's parties
And what will she do with Thursday's rags
When Monday comes around
She'll turn once more to Sunday's clown and cry behind the door

And what costume shall the poor girl wear
To all tomorrow's parties
For Thursday's child is Sunday's clown
For whom none will go mourning

A blackened shroud
A hand-me-down gown
Of rags and silks—a costume
Fit for one who sits and cries
For all tomorrow's parties

Heroin

I don't know just where I'm going
But I'm gonna try for the kingdom if I can
'Cause it makes me feel like I'm a man
When I put a spike into my vein
Then I tell you things aren't quite the same
When I'm rushin' on my run
And I feel just like Jesus' son
And I guess that I just don't know
And I guess that I just don't know

I have made a big decision
I'm gonna try to nullify my life
'Cause when the blood begins to flow
When it shoots up the dropper's neck
When I'm closing in on death
You can't help me, not you guys
Or all you sweet girls with all your sweet talk
You can all go take a walk
And I guess that I just don't know
And I guess that I just don't know

I wish that I was born a thousand years ago
I wish that I'd sailed the darkened seas
On a great big clipper ship
Going from this land here to that
Ah, in a sailor's suit and cap
Away from the big city

Where a man cannot be free
Of all the evils of this town
And of himself and those around
And I guess that I just don't know
And I guess that I just don't know

Heroin, be the death of me
Heroin, it's my wife and it's my life
Because a mainer to my vein
Leads to a center in my head
And then I'm better off than dead
Because when the smack begins to flow
I really don't care any more
About all the Jim-Jims in this town
And all the politicians making crazy sounds
And everybody putting everybody else down
And all the dead bodies piled up in mounds

'Cause when the smack begins to flow
Then I really don't care any more
Ah when that heroin is in my blood
And that blood is in my head
Man thank God I'm good as dead
And thank your God that I'm not aware
And thank God that I just don't care
And I guess that I just don't know
Oh and I guess that I just don't know

There She Goes Again

There she goes again
She's out on the streets again
She's down on her knees my friend
But you know she'll never ask you please again
Now take a look, there's no tears in her eyes
She won't take it from just any guy
What can you do
You see her walking on down the street
Look at all your friends that she's gonna meet
You'd better hit her

There she goes again
She's knocked out on her feet again
She's down on her knees my friend
You know she'll never ask you please again
Now take a look, there's no tears in her eyes
Like a bird, you know she will fly
What can you do
You see her walking on down the street
Look at all your friends that she's gonna meet (there she goes)
You'd better hit her

I'll Be Your Mirror

I'll be your mirror, reflect what you are
In case you don't know
I'll be the wind, the rain, and the sunset
The light on your door
To show that you're home

When you think the night has seen your mind
That inside you're twisted and unkind
Let me stand to show that you are blind
Please put down your hands
'Cause I see you

I find it hard
To believe you don't know
The beauty you are
But if you don't,
Let me be your eyes
A hand to your darkness
So you won't be afraid

When you think the night has seen your mind
That inside you're twisted and unkind
Let me stand to show that you are blind
Please put down your hands
'Cause I see you

I'll be your mirror

Black Angel's Death Song

The myriad choices of his fate set themselves out upon
A plate for him to choose, what had he to lose
Not a ghost-bloodied country all covered with sleep
Where the black angel did weep
Not an old city street in the east
Gone to choose

And wandering's brother walked on through the night
With his hair
In his face
Long a long splintered cut from the knife of G.T.

The Rally Man's patter ran on through the dawn
Until we said so long to his skull
Shrill yell

Shining brightly, red-rimmed and red-lined with the time
Effused with the choice of the mind on ice skates scraping chunks
From the bells

Cut mouth bleeding razors forget in the pain
Antiseptic remains coo goodbye
So you fly
To the cozy brown snow of the east
Gone to choose, choose again

Sacrificials remain make it hard to forget
Where you come from
The stools of your eyes serve to realize pain
Choose again

Roberman's refrain of the sacrilege recluse
For the loss of a horse
Went the bowels in the tail of a rat
Come again, choose to go

And if epiphanies terror reduced you to shame
Have your head bobbed and weaved
Choose a side
To be on

If the stone glances off split didactics in two
Lay the colour of mouse trails all's green try between
If you choose
If you choose
Try to lose
For the loss of remain come and start
Start the game
I Chi–Chi
Chi Chi I
Chi Chi Chi
Ka–Ta–Ko
Choose to choose
Choose to choose
Choose to go

European Son

You killed your European Son
You spit on those under twenty-one
But now your blue clouds have gone
You'd better say so long
Hey hey, bye bye bye

You made your wallpapers green
You want to make love to the scene
Your European Son is gone
You'd better say so long
Your clouds driftin' good-bye

V6-5046
STEREO
WHITE LIGHT/WHITE HEAT
Verve
THE VELVET UNDERGROUND

White Light/White Heat

White Light
Goin' messin' up my mind
White Light
Don't you know it's gonna make me go blind
White Heat
White Heat
It tickle me down to my toes
White Light
Lord have mercy White Light have it goodness knows

White Light
White Light
Goin' messin' up my brain
White Light
Oh, White Light
It's gonna drive me insane
White Heat
White Heat it tickle me down to my toes
White Light
Oh, White Light I said now, goodness knows, do it
White Light
Oh, I surely do love to watch that stuff drip itself in
White Light
Watch that side, watch that side
Don't you know gonna be dead and dried
White Heat
Yeah foxy momma watchin' me walkin' down the street
White Light
Come upside your head, gonna make you dead hang on your street

White Light
Movin' me between my brain
White Light
Gonna make you go insane
White Heat
Oh, White Heat it tickles me down to my toes
White Light
Oh White Light, I said now, goodness knows
White Light
Oh, White Light it lightens up my eyes
White Light
Don't you know it fills me up with surprise
White Heat
Oh, White Heat tickle me down to my toes
White Light
Oh, White Light, I'll tell you now, goodness knows, now work it
White Light
Oh, she surely do move speed
Watch that speedfreak, watch that speedfreak
Yeah we're gonna go and make it every week
White Heat
Oh, sputter mutter, everybody's gonna go and kill their mother

White Light
Here she comes, here she comes
Everybody get it gonna make me run
Do it

The Gift

Waldo Jeffers had reached his limit. It was now mid-August, which meant he had been separated from Marsha for more than two months. Two months, and all he had to show were three dog-eared letters and two very expensive long-distance phone calls. True, when school had ended and she'd returned to Wisconsin and he to Locust, Pennsylvania, she had sworn to maintain a certain fidelity. She would date occasionally, but merely as amusement. She would remain faithful.

But lately, Waldo had begun to worry. He had trouble sleeping at night, and when he did, he had horrible dreams. He lay awake at night, tossing and turning underneath his pleated quilt protector, tears welling in his eyes as he pictured Marsha, her sworn vows overcome by liquor and the smooth soothing of some Neanderthal, finally submitting to the final caresses of sexual oblivion. It was more than the human mind could bear.

Visions of Marsha's faithlessness haunted him. Daytime fantasies of sexual abandon permeated his thoughts, and the thing was, they wouldn't understand how she really was. He, Waldo, alone understood this. He had intuitively grasped every nook and cranny of her psyche. He had made her smile—she needed him, and he wasn't there. (ahh....)

The idea came to him on the Thursday before the Mummers' parade was scheduled to appear. He'd just finished mowing and edging the Edison's lawn for a dollar fifty and then checked the mailbox to see if there was at least a word from Marsha. There was nothing but a circular from the Amalgamated Aluminum Company of America inquiring into his awning needs. At least they cared enough to write. It was a New York company. You could go anywhere in the mails.

Then it struck him. He didn't have enough money to go to Wisconsin in the accepted fashion, true, but why not mail himself? It was absurdly simple. He would ship himself, parcel-post special delivery. The next day Waldo went to the supermarket to purchase the necessary equipment. He bought masking tape, a staple-gun, and a medium sized cardboard box, just right for a person of his build. He judged that with a minimum of jostling, he could ride quite comfortably. A few airholes, some water, and perhaps midnight snacks, and it would probably be as good as going tourist.

By Friday afternoon, Waldo was set. He was thoroughly packed and the post office had agreed to pick him up at three o'clock. He had marked the package "fragile" and as he sat curled up inside, resting on the foam-rubber cushioning he'd thoughtfully included, he tried to picture the look of awe and happiness on Marsha's face, as she opened her door, saw the package, tipped the deliverer, and then opened it to see her Waldo finally there in person. She would kiss him, and then maybe they could see a movie. If he'd only thought of this before. Suddenly, rough hands gripped his package, and he found himself borne up. He landed with a thud in a truck and was off.

Marsha Bronson had just finished setting her hair. It had been a very rough weekend. She had to remember not to drink like that. Bill had been nice about it, though. After it was over, he'd said he still respected her, and after all it was certainly the way of nature, and even though, no, he didn't love her, he did feel an affection for her. And after all, they were grown adults. Oh, what Bill could teach Waldo. But that seemed many years ago.

Sheila Klein, her very, very best friend walked in through the porch screen door and into the kitchen.

"Oh god, it's absolutely maudlin outside."

"I know what you mean, I feel all icky." Marsha tightened the belt on her cotton robe with the silk outer edge. Sheila ran her finger over some salt grains on the kitchen table, licked her finger and made a face.

"I'm supposed to be taking these salt pills, but"—she wrinkled her nose—"they make me feel like throwing up."

Marsha started to pat herself under the chin, an exercise she had seen on television. "God, don't even talk about that." She got up from the table and went to the sink, where she picked up a bottle of pink and blue vitamins. "Want one? Supposed to be better than steak," and then attempted to touch her knees.

"I don't think I'll ever touch a daiquiri again." She gave up and sat down, this time nearer the small table that supported the telephone. "Maybe Bill will call," she said to Sheila's glance. Sheila nibbled on her cuticle.

"After last night, I thought maybe you'd be through with him."

"I know what you mean. My god, he was like an octopus—hands all over the place!" she gestured raising her arms upward in defense. "The thing is, after a while you get tired of fighting with him, you know, and after all I didn't really do anything Friday and Saturday, so I kind of owed it to him—you know what I mean." She started to scratch.

Sheila was giggling with her hand over her mouth. "I tell you, I felt the same way and even, after a while," here she bent forward in a whisper, "I wanted to." Now she was laughing very loudly.

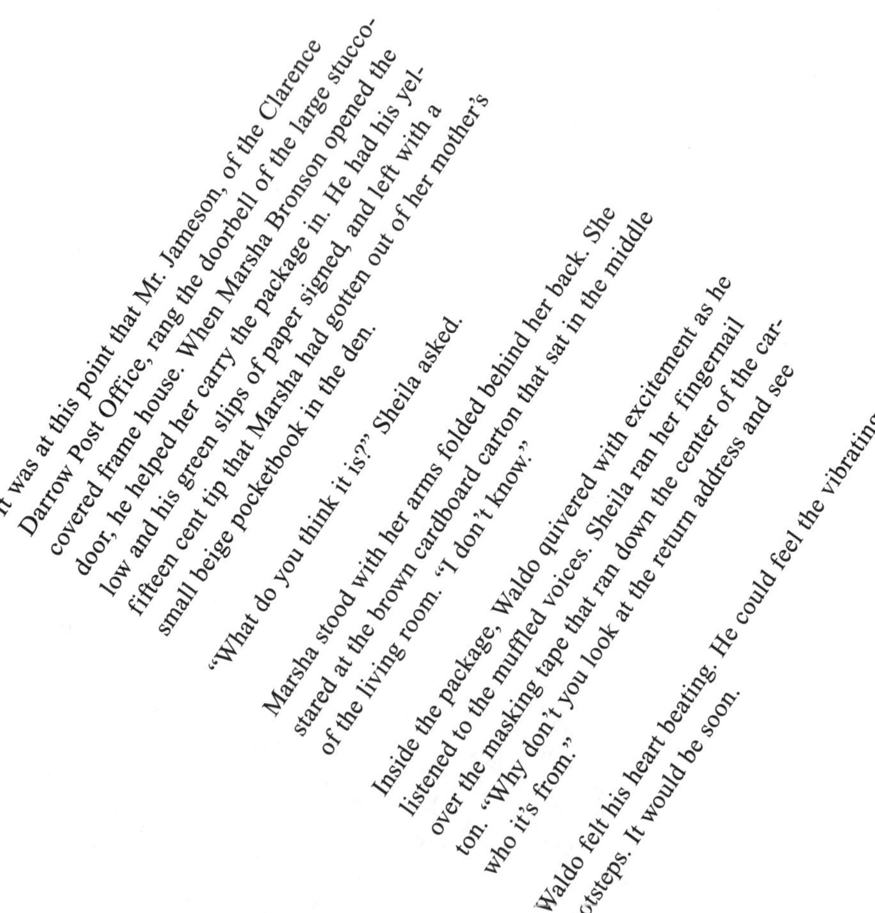

It was at this point that Mr. Jameson, of the Clarence Darrow Post Office, rang the doorbell of the large stucco-covered frame house. When Marsha Bronson opened the door, he helped her carry the package in. He had his yellow and his green slips of paper signed, and left with a fifteen cent tip that Marsha had gotten out of her mother's small beige pocketbook in the den.

"What do you think it is?" Sheila asked.

Marsha stood with her arms folded behind her back. She stared at the brown cardboard carton that sat in the middle of the living room. "I don't know."

Inside the package, Waldo quivered with excitement as he listened to the muffled voices. Sheila ran her fingernail over the masking tape that ran down the center of the carton. "Why don't you look at the return address and see who it's from."

Waldo felt his heart beating. He could feel the vibrating footsteps. It would be soon.

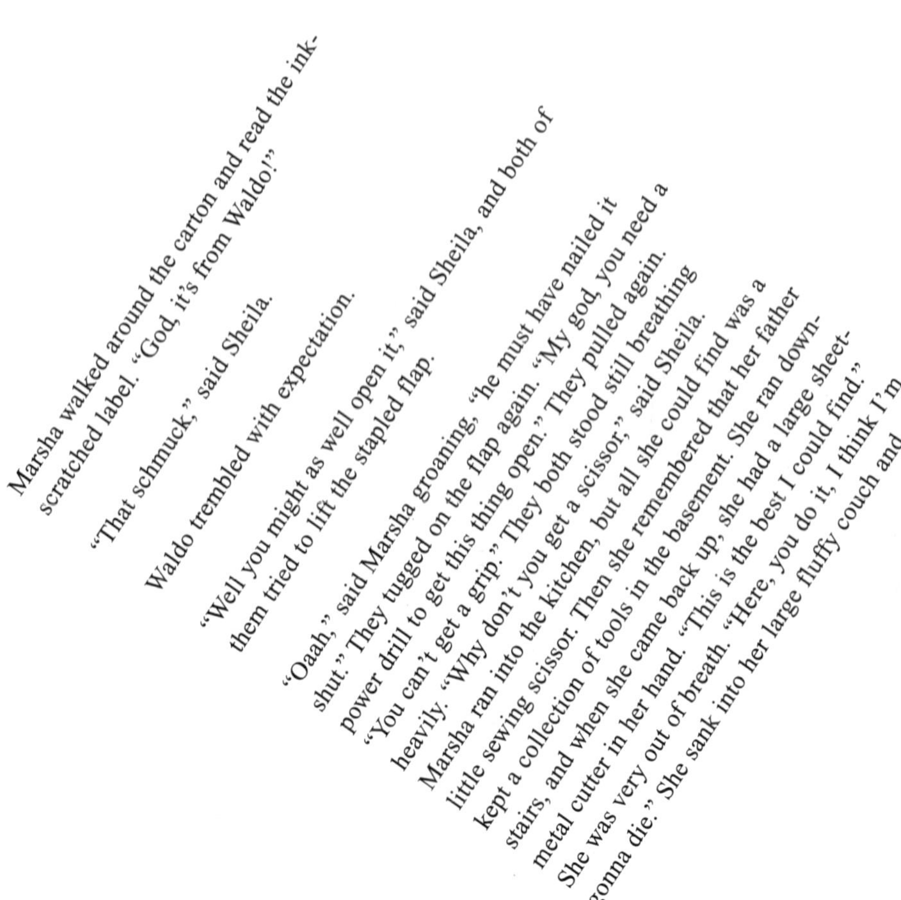

Marsha walked around the carton and read the ink-scratched label. "God, it's from Waldo!"

"That schmuck," said Sheila.

Waldo trembled with expectation.

"Well you might as well open it," said Sheila, and both of them tried to lift the stapled flap.

"Oaah," said Marsha groaning, "he must have nailed it shut." They tugged on the flap again. "My god, you need a power drill to get this thing open." They pulled again. "You can't get a grip." They both stood still breathing heavily. "Why don't you get a scissor," said Sheila. Marsha ran into the kitchen, but all she could find was a little sewing scissor. Then she remembered that her father kept a collection of tools in the basement. She ran downstairs, and when she came back up, she had a large sheet-metal cutter in her hand. "This is the best I could find." She was very out of breath. "Here, you do it, I think I'm gonna die." She sank into her large fluffy couch and exhaled noisily. Sheila tried to make a slit between the masking tape and the end of the cardboard flap, but the blade was too big and there wasn't enough room. "Goddamn this thing," she said feeling very exasperated. Then, smiling, "I got an idea." "What?" said Marsha. "Just watch," said Sheila, touching her finger to her head.

Inside the package, Waldo was so transfixed with excitement that he could barely breathe. His skin felt prickly from the heat and he could feel his heart beating in his throat. It would be soon.

Sheila stood quite upright and walked around to the other side of the package. Then she sank down to her knees, grasped the cutter by both handles, took a deep breath, and plunged the long blade through the middle of the package, through the masking tape, through the cardboard, through the cushioning, and right through the center of Waldo Jeffers' head, which split slightly and caused little rhythmic arcs of red to pulsate gently in the morning sun.

Lady Godiva dressed so demurely
Pats the head of another curly-haired boy
Just another toy
Sick with silence she weeps sincerely
Saying words that have oh so clearly been said
So long ago

Draperies wrapped gently 'round her shoulder
Life has made her that much bolder now
That she found out how

Dressed in silk, Latin lace and envy
Pride and joy of the latest penny feire
Pretty passing care

Hair today now dipped in the water
Making love to every poor daughter's son
Isn't it fun

Now today propping grace with envy
Lady Godiva peers to see if anyone's there
And hasn't a care

Doctor is coming the nurse thinks SWEETLY
Turning on the machines that NEATLY pump air
The body lies bare

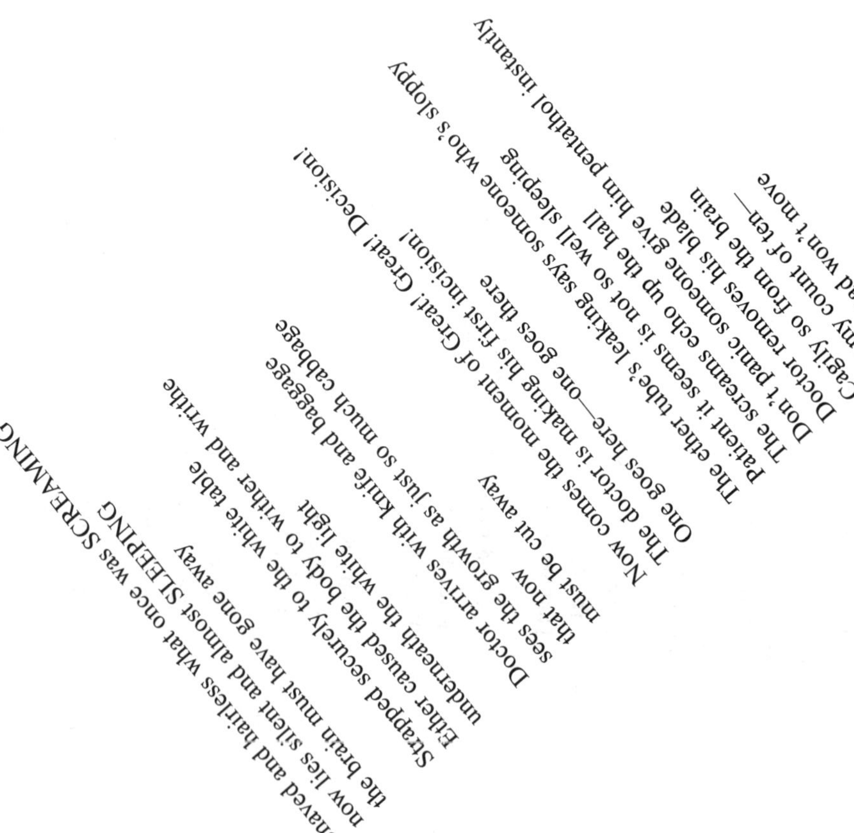

Shaved and hairless what once was SCREAMING
now lies silent and almost SLEEPING
the brain must have gone away

Strapped securely to the white table
Ether caused the body to wither and writhe
underneath the white light

Doctor arrives with knife and baggage
sees the growth as just so much cabbage
that now
must be cut away

Now comes the moment of Great! Great! Decision!
The doctor is making his first incision!
One goes here—one goes there

The ether tube's leaking says someone who's sloppy
Patient it seems is not so well sleeping
The screams echo up the hall
Don't panic someone give him pentathol instantly
Doctor removes his blade
Cagily so from the brain
By my count of ten—
head won't move

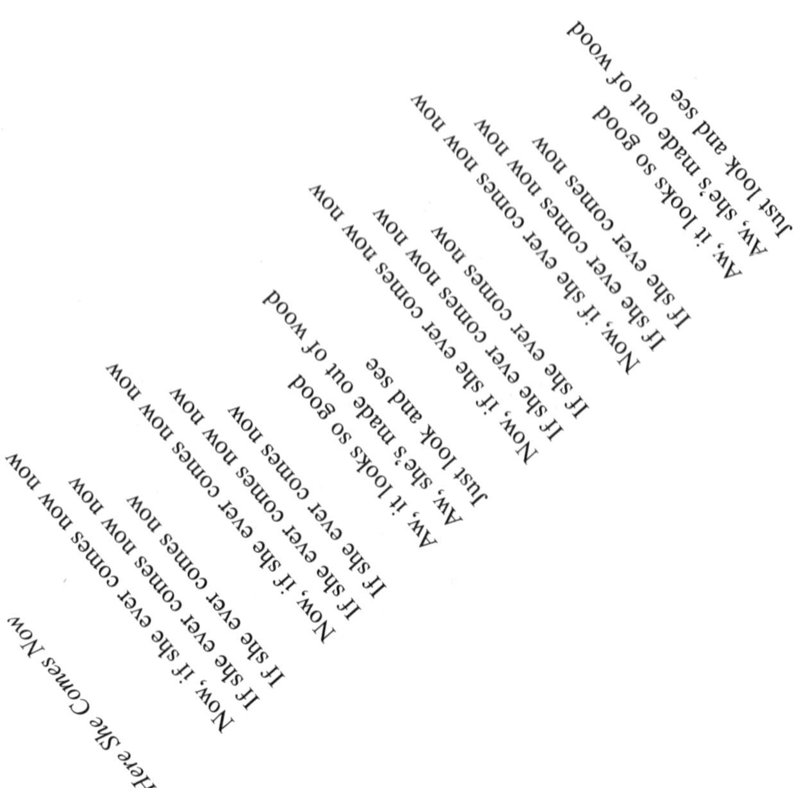

Here She Comes Now

Now, if she ever comes now now
If she ever comes now now
If she ever comes now
Now, if she ever comes now now
If she ever comes now now
If she ever comes now
Aw, it looks so good
Aw, she's made out of wood
Just look and see

Now, if she ever comes now now
If she ever comes now now
If she ever comes now
Now, if she ever comes now now
If she ever comes now now
If she ever comes now
Aw, it looks so good
Aw, she's made out of wood
Just look and see

I Heard Her Call My Name

Here comes the count-down
It's gone gone gone, baby
Got my eyes wide open
Ever since I was crippled on Monday
Got my eyeballs on my knees, a baby-walking
I rapped for hours with Mad Mary Williams
She said she never understood a word from me because
I know that she cares about me
I heard her call my name
And I know that she's long dead and gone
Still it ain't the same
When I wake up in this morning, mama
I heard her call my name
I know she's dead and long, long gone
I heard her call my name
And then I felt my mind split open

Sister Ray

Duck and Sally inside
They're cookin' for the down five
Who's starin' at Miss Rayon
Who's busy lickin' up her pigpen
I'm searchin' for my mainline
I said I couldn't hit it sideways
I said I couldn't hit it sideways
Aw, just like Sister Ray said
Whip it on

Rosie and Miss Rayon
They're busy waitin' for her booster
Who just got back from Carolina
She said she didn't like the weather
They're busy waitin' for her sailor
Who's drinking dressed in pink and leather
He's just here from Alabama
He wants to know a way to earn a dollar
I'm searchin' for my mainer
I said I couldn't hit it sideways
I couldn't hit it sideways
Aw, just like Sister Ray said
Play it on

Cecil's got his new piece
He cocks and shoots it between three and four
He aims it at the sailor
Shoots him down dead on the floor
Aw, you shouldn't do that

Don’t you know you’ll stain the carpet
Now don’t you know you’ll stain the carpet
And by the way have you got a dollar
Oh, no man, I haven’t got the time-time
Too busy sucking on a ding-dong
Too busy sucking on my ding-dong
Aw, she does just like Sister Ray says

I am searchin’ for my mainline
I said I c-c-couldn’t hit it sideways
I c-c-c-c-couldn’t hit it sideways
Oh, do it, do it, aw just just just just like Sister Ray said

Now who is that knocking?
Who’s knocking at my chamber door
Could it be the police
They come and take me for a ride-ride
Oh but I haven’t got the time-time
Hey, hey, hey she’s busy sucking on my ding-dong
She’s busy sucking on my ding-dong
Aw now do it just like Sister Ray says

I’m searchin’ for my mainline
I couldn’t hit it sideways
I couldn’t hit it sideways
Now just like, oh just like aw, just like Sister Ray said

Whip it on me Jim!

THE VELVET UNDERGROUND

Candy Says

Candy says I've come to hate my body
And all that it requires in this world
Candy says I'd like to know completely
What others so discreetly talk about

Candy says I hate the quiet places
That cause the smallest taste of what will be
Candy says I hate the big decisions
That cause endless revisions in my mind

I'm gonna watch the blue birds fly
Over my shoulder
I'm gonna watch them pass me by
Maybe when I'm older
What do you think I'd see
If I could walk away from me

What Goes On

What goes on here in your mind
I think that I am falling down
What goes on here in your mind
I think that I am upside down
Lady, be good and do what you should
You know it'll work alright
Lady, be good and do what you should
You know it'll be alright

I'm goin up and I'm goin' down
I'm gonna fly from side to side
See the bells up in the sky
Somebody's cut the string in two
Lady, be good and do what you should
You know it'll work alright
Lady, be good and do what you should
You know it'll be it alright

One minute one one minute two
One minute up and one minute down
What goes on here in your mind
I think that I am falling down
Lady, be good do what you should
You know it'll work alright
Lady, be good do what you should
You know it'll be alright

Some Kinda Love

Some kinda love
Marguerita told Tom
Between thought and expression lies a lifetime
Situations arise because of the weather
And no kinds of love
Are better than others

Some kinds of love
Marguerita told Tom
Like a dirty French novel
Combines the absurd with the vulgar
And some kinds of love
The possibilities are endless
And for me to miss one
Would seem to be groundless

I heard what you said
Marguerita heard Tom
And of course you're a bore
But in that you're not charmless
'Cause a bore is a straight line
That finds a wealth in division
And some kinds of love
Are mistaken for vision

Put jelly on your shoulder
Let us do what you fear most
That from which you recoil
But which still makes your eyes moist

Put jelly on your shoulder, baby
Lie down upon the carpet
Between thought and expression
Let us now kiss the culprit

I don't know just what it's all about
Put on your red pajamas and find out

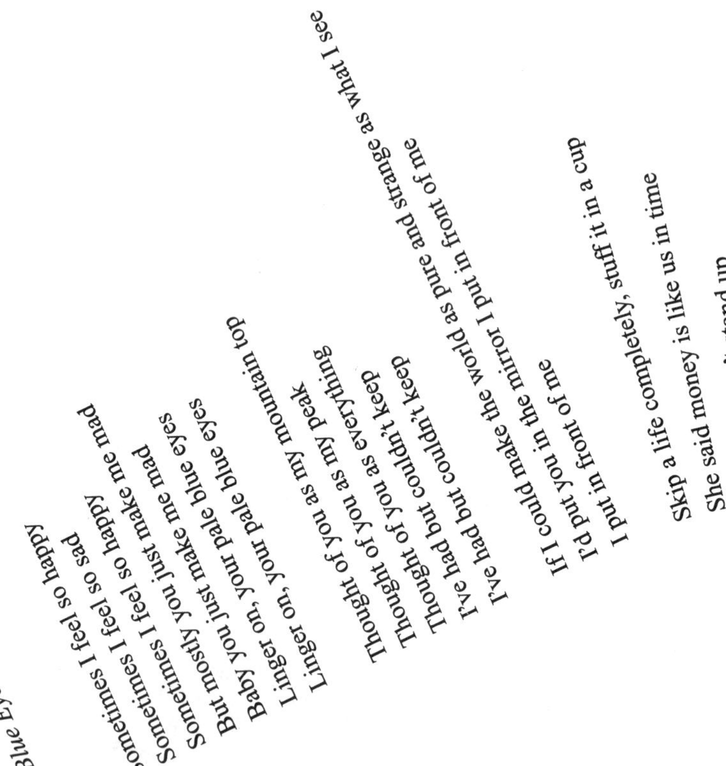

Pale Blue Eyes

Sometimes I feel so happy
Sometimes I feel so sad
Sometimes I feel so happy
Sometimes I feel so happy me mad
Sometimes I just make me mad
Sometimes you just make me eyes
Sometimes you just make me blue eyes
But mostly you just make me blue eyes
Baby you just your pale blue eyes
Linger on, your pale blue eyes

Thought of you as my mountain top
Thought of you as my peak
Thought of you as everything
I've had but couldn't keep
I've had but couldn't keep

If I could make the world as pure and strange as what I see
I'd put you in the mirror I put in front of me
I'd put you in front of me

Skip a life completely, stuff it in a cup
She said money is like us in time
It lies but can't stand up

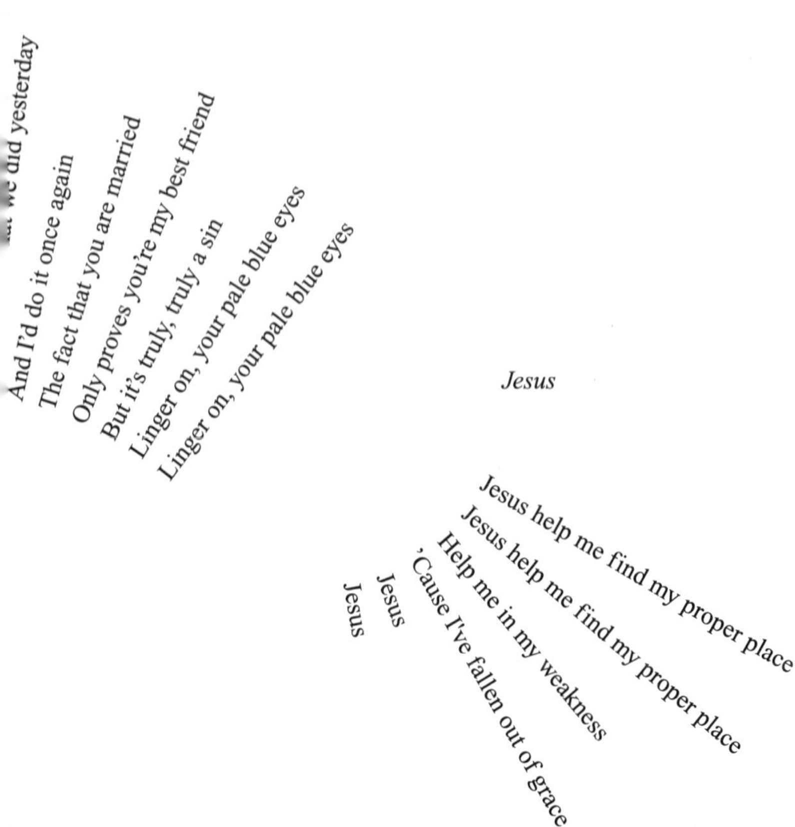
we did yesterday
And I'd do it once again
The fact that you are married
Only proves you're my best friend
But it's truly, truly a sin
Linger on, your pale blue eyes
Linger on, your pale blue eyes
Jesus
Jesus help me find my proper place
Jesus help me find my proper place
Help me in my weakness
'Cause I've fallen out of grace
Jesus
Jesus

Beginning to See the Light

I'm beginning to see the light
I'm beginning to see the light
Some people work very hard
But still they never get it right
I'm beginning to see the light

I'm beginning to see the light
Now I'm beginning to see the light
Wine in the morning and some breakfast at night
I'm beginning to see the light

Here we go again
Playing the fool again
Here we go again
Acting hard again

I'm beginning to see the light
I'm beginning to see the light
I wore my teeth in my hands
So I could mess the hair of the night
Well I'm beginning to see the light

I met myself in a dream
And I just wanted to tell you—everything was all right
I'm beginning to see the light

Here comes two of you

Which one will you choose?

One is black and one is blue

Don't know just what to do

I'm beginning to see the light
I'm beginning to see the light
Some people work very hard
But still they never get it right
Well I'm beginning to see the light

There are problems in these times
But none of them are mine
Baby, I'm beginning to see the light

Here we go again
I thought that you were my friend
Here we go again
I thought that you were my friend

How does it feel to be loved?

I'm Set Free

I've been set free and I've been bound
To the memories of yesterday's clowns
I've been set free and I've been bound and now
I'm set free
I'm set free
I'm set free to find a new illusion

I've been blinded but now I can see
What in the world has happened to me
The prince of stories who walks right by me and now
I'm set free
I'm set free
I'm set free to find a new illusion

I've been set free and I've been bound
Let me tell you people what I've found
I saw my head laughing, rolling on the ground and now
I'm set free
I'm set free
I'm set free to find a new illusion

That's the Story of My Life

That's the story of my life
That's the difference between wrong and right
But Billy said, both those words are dead
That's the story of my life

The Murder Mystery

A

candy screen wrappers of silkscreen fantastic, requiring memories, both lovely and guilt-free, lurid and lovely with twilight of ages, luscious and lovely and filthy with laughter, laconic giggles, ennui for the passion, in order to justify most spurious desires, rectify moments, most serious and urgent, to hail upon the face of most odious time, requiring replies most facile and vacuous, with words nearly singed, with the heartbeat of passions, spew forth with the grace of a tart going under, subject of great concern, noble origin

B

[denigrate obtuse and active verbs pronouns, skewer the sieve of the optical sewer, release the handle that holds all the gates up, puncture the eyeballs, that seep all the muck up, read all the books and the people worth reading and still see the muck on the sky of the ceiling]

A

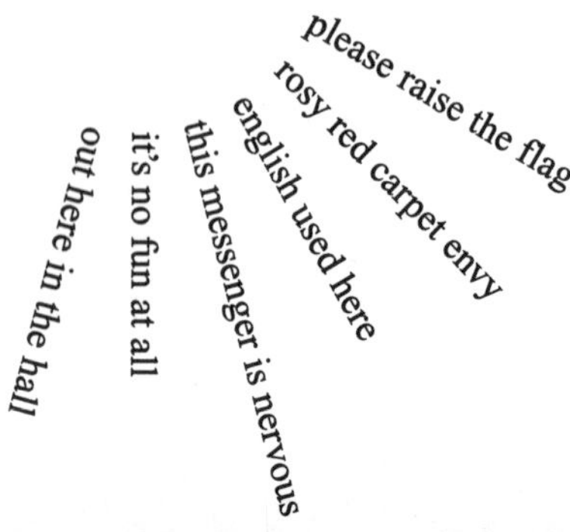

please raise the flag
rosy red carpet envy
english used here
this messenger is nervous
it's no fun at all
out here in the hall

B

[mister moonlight
succulent smooth and gorgeous
Isn't it nice? We're number one and so forth
Isn't it sweet being unique?]

A

for screeching and yelling and various offenses, lower the queen and bend her over the tub, against the state, the country, the committee, hold her head under the water please for an hour, for groveling and spewing and various offenses, puncture that bloat with the wing of a sparrow, the inverse, the obverse, the converse, the reverse, the sharpening wing of the edge of a sparrow, for suitable reckonings too numerous to mention, as the queen is fat she is devoured by rats, there is one way to skin a cat or poison a rat it is here to four hear to three forthrightly stated

put down that rag simpering, callow and morose
who let you in?
if I knew, then I could get out
the murder you see
is a mystery to me

B

[relent and obverse and inverse and perverse and reverse the
inverse of perverse and reverse and reverse and reverse and
reverse and chop it and pluck it and cut it and spit
it and sew it to joy on the edge of a cyclops and spinet it to
rage on the edge of a cylindrical minute]

[dear Mister Muse
fellow of wit and gentry
medieval ruse
filling the shallow and
empty, fools that duel
duel in pools]

A

to Rembrandt and Oswald, to peanuts and ketchup,
sanctimonious sycophants stir in the bushes, up to the stand
with your foot on the bible as king I must order and constantly
arouse, if you swear to catch up and throw up and up up, a
king full of virgin and kiss me and spin it, excuse me to
willow and wander dark wonders, divest me of robes-suture
Harry and pig meat, the fate of a nation, rests hard on your
bosoms, the king on his throne, puts his hand down his robe,
the torture of inverse and silk screen and Harry, and set the
tongue squealing the reverse and inverse

B

[tantalize poets with visions of grandeur, their faces turn blue
with the reek of the compost, as the living try hard to retain
what the dead lost, with double dead sickness from writing at
what cost and business and business and reverse and reverse
and set the brain reeling the inverse and perverse]

A

objections suffice
apelike and tactile bassoon
oboeing me
cordon the virus' section
off to the left
is what is not right

B

[English arcane
tantamount here to frenzy
passing for me
lascivious elder passion
corpulent filth
disguised as silk]

A

contempt, contempt, and contempt for the boredom, I shall poison the city and sink it with fire, for Cordless and Harry and Apepig and Scissor, the messenger's wig seems fraught with desire, for blueberry picnics, and pince-nez and magpies, the messenger's skirt, would you please hook it higher, for children and adults all those under 90, how truly disgusting! would you please put it down? A stray in this fray is no condom worth saving, as king I'm quite just, but it's just quite impossible, a robe and a robe and a robe and a bat, no double class inverse could make lying worth dying

B

[with cheap simian melodies, hillbilly outgush, for illiterate ramblings for cheap understandings, for mass understanding the simple the inverse, the compost, the reverse, the obtuse and stupid, and business, and business, and cheap, stupid lyrics, and simple mass reverse while the real thing is dying]

A

accept the pig, enter the Owl and Gorgeous, King on the left,

it on the right and primping adjusting his nose as he reads

from his scroll
off with his head, take his head from his neck off, requiring memories both lovely and guilt-free, put out his eyes, then cut his nose off, sanctimonious synchophants stir in the bushes, scoop out his brain, put a string where his ears were, all the king's horses and all the king's men, swing the whole mess at the end of the wire, scratch out his eyes with the tip of a razor, let the wire extend from the tip of a rose, Caroline, Caroline, Caroline, Oh! but retain the remnants of what once was a nose, pass me my robe, fill my bath up with water

B

[folksy knockwurst peel back the skin of French and what do you find? follicles intertwining, succulent prose wrapped up in robes]

[jumpsuit and pig meat and making his fortune, while making them happy with the inverse and obverse and making them happy and making them happy with the coy and the stupid, just another dumb lackey, who puts out the one thing, while singing the other, but the real thing's alone and it is no man's brother]

A

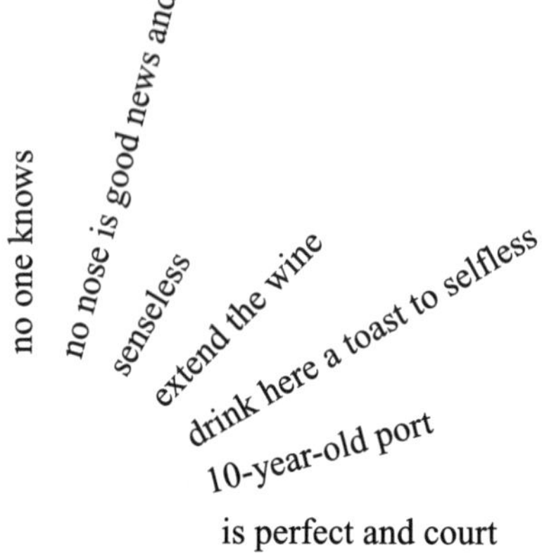
no one knows
no nose is good news and
senseless
extend the wine
drink here a toast to selfless
10-year-old port
is perfect and court

B

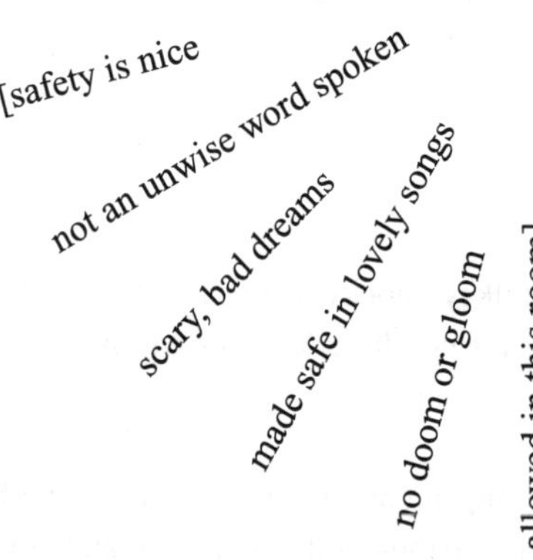
[safety is nice
not an unwise word spoken
scary, bad dreams
made safe in lovely songs
no doom or gloom
allowed in this room]

A

Casbah and Cascade and Rosehip and Feeling, Cascade and Cyanide, Rachmaninoff, Beethoven-skull silly wagon and justice and perverse and reverse the inverse and inverse and inverse, blueberry catalog, questionable earnings, hustler's lament and the rest will in due cry, to battle and scramble and browbeat and hurt while chewing on minstrels and choking on dirt, disease please seems the order of the day, please the king, please the king, please the king day, Casbah and Cascade and Rosehip and Feeling, point of order return the kings here to the ceiling

razzamatazz,
there's nothing on my shoulder, lust is a must, shaving my
head's made me bolder, will you kindly read what it was I
brought thee

B

[oh, not to be whistled or studied or hummed or remembered at nights, when the I is alone, but to skewer and ravage and savage and split with the grace of a diamond and bellicose wit, to stun and to stagger with words as such stone, that those who do hear cannot again return home]

[hello to Ray
hello to Godiva and Angel who
let you in?
isn't it nice, the party?
aren't the lights pretty at night?]

A

sick leaf and sorrow and pincers net-scissors, regard and refrain from the daughters of marriage, regards for the elders and youngest in carriage, regard and regard for the inverse and perverse and obverse, and diverse, of reverse and reverse, regard from the sick, the dumb, and the camel from pump's storing water, like brain is to marrow to x-ray and filthy and cutting and peeling to skin and to skin and to bone into structure to livid and pallid and turgid and structured and structured and structured and structured and structured and regard and refrain and regard and refrain, the sick, and the dumb, inverse, reverse and perverse

B

[contempt, contempt, and contempt for the seething, for writhing and reeling and two-bit reportage, for sick with the body and sinister holy, the drowned burst blue babies now dead on the seashore, the valorous horsemen, who hang from the ceiling, the pig on the carpet, the dusty pale jissom, that has no effect for the sick with the see-saw, the inverse, obverse, converse, reverse of reverse the diverse and converse of reverse and perverse and sweet pyrotechnics, and let's have another of inverse, converse, diverse, perverse, and reverse, *hell's graveyard is damned as they chew on their brains, the slick and the scum, reverse, inverse and perverse]*

A

plowing while it's done away
dumb and ready pig meat
sick upon the carpet
climb into the casket
safe within the parapet
sack is in the parapet
pigs are out and growling
slaughter by the seashore
see the lifeguard drowning
sea is full of fishes
fish's full of china
china plates are falling
all fall down
sick and shiny carpet
lie before my eyes eyes
lead me to the ceiling
walk upon the wall wall
tender as the green grass
drink the whisky horror
see the young girls dancing
flies upon the beaches
beaches are for sailors
nuns across the sea-wall
black hood horseman raging
swordsman eating fire

B

[sick upon the staircase
sick upon the carpet
blood upon the pillow
climb into the parapet
see the church bells gleaming
knife that scrapes a sick plate
dentures full of air holes
the tailor couldn't mend straight
shoot her full of air holes
climbing up the casket
take me to the casket
teeth upon her red throat
screw me in the daisies
rip apart her holler
snip the seas fantastic
treat her like a sailor
full and free and nervous
out to make his fortune
either this or that way
sickly or in good health
piss upon a building
like a dog in training
teach to heel or holler
yodel on a sing song
down upon the carpet]

A

fire on the carpet
set the house ablazing
seize and bring it flaming
gently to the ground ground
Dizzy Bell Miss Fortune
fat and full of love-juice
drip it on the carpet
down below the fire hose
weep and whisky fortune
sail me to the moon, dear
drunken dungeon sailors
headless Roman horsemen
the king and queen are empty
their heads are in the outhouse
fish upon the water
bowl upon the saviour
toothless wigged Laureate
plain and full of fancy
name upon a letterhead
impressing all the wheatgerm
love you for a nickel
ball you for a quarter
set the casket flaming
do not go gentle blazing

B

[tickle polyester
sick within the parapet
screwing for a dollar
sucking on a fire-hose
chewing on a rubber line
tied to chairs and rare bits
pay another player
oh you're such a good lad
here's another dollar
tie him to the bedpost
sick with witches' covens
craving for a raw meat
bones upon the metal
sick upon the circle
down upon the carpet
down below the parapet
waiting for your bidding
pig upon the carpet
tumescent railroad
neuro-anaesthesia analog
ready for a good look
drooling at the birches
swinging from the birches
succulent Nebraska]

After Hours

If you close the door, the night could last forever
Leave the sunshine out and say hello to never
All the people are dancing and they're having such fun
I wish it could happen to me
But if you close the door, I'd never have to see the day again

If you close the door, the night could last forever
Leave the wine glass out and drink a toast to never
Oh, someday I know someone will look into my eyes
And say hello—you're my very special one—
But if you close the door I'd never have to see the day again

Dark party bars
Shiny Cadillac cars
And the people on subways and trains
Looking gray in the rain
As they stand disarrayed
Oh but people look well in the dark

And if you close the door the night could last forever
Leave the sunshine out and say hello to never
All the people are dancing and they're having such fun
I wish it could happen to me
'Cause if you close the door I'd never have to see the day again
I'd never have to see the day again

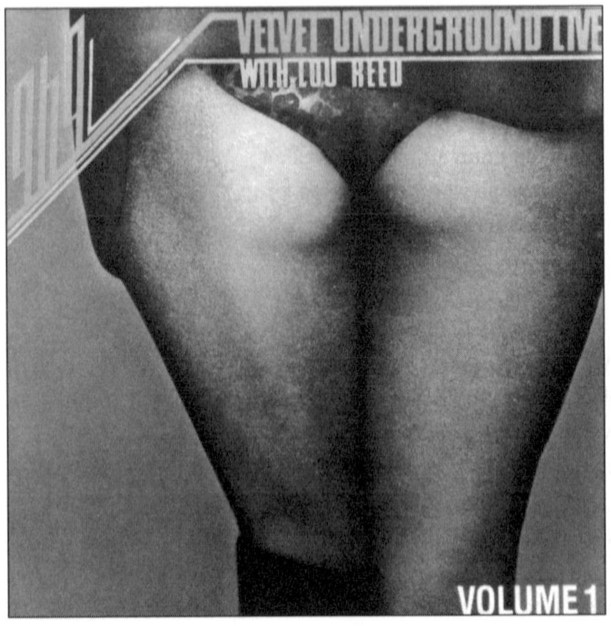
VELVET UNDERGROUND LIVE
WITH LOU REED
VOLUME 1

Sweet Jane (Prototype)

Anyone who ever had a heart
Wouldn't turn around and break it
And anyone who's ever played a part
Wouldn't turn around and hate it

Sweet Jane

Waiting for Jimmy down by the alley
Waitin' there for him to come home
Waitin' down on another corner
Figurin' ways to get back home

Sweet Jane

Anyone who ever had a dream
Anyone who's ever played a part
Anyone who's gonna live lonely
Anyone who's ever split apart

Sweet Jane

Heavenly wine and roses
Seem to whisper to me
When you smile

Sweet Jane

New Age (Prototype)

Waiting for the phone to ring
Diamond necklace on my shoulder
Waiting for the phone to ring
Lipstick on my neck and shoulder
It seems to be my fancy
To make it with Frank and Nancy when
Over the bridge we go, looking for love
Over the bridge we go
Looking for love

I'll come running to you
Hey baby, if you want me
I'll come running to you
Baby, if you want me

Looking at my hands today
Looked to me that they're made of ivory
Had a funny call today
Someone died and someone's married
You know that it's my fancy
To make it with Frank and Nancy when
Over the bridge they go, looking for love
Over the bridge we go
Looking for love

I'll come running to you
Hey baby, if you want me
I'll come running to you
Baby, if you want me
Something's got a hold on me
And I don't know what
Something's got a hold on me
And I don't know what

It's the beginning of a new age

Over You

Here I go again
Just gonna play it like a fool again
Here I go again
Over you, over you

I'm just like a bell again
You know I'm starting to ring again
Here I go again
Over you, over you

Typically when I had it
Treated it like dirt
Now naturally, when I don't have it
I am chasing less and less rainbows

THE VELVET UNDERGROUND LOADED

Who Loves the Sun

Who loves the sun, who cares that it makes plants grow
Who cares what it does since you broke my heart
Who loves the wind, who cares that it makes breezes
Who cares what it does since you broke my heart
Who loves the sun
Who loves the sun
Not everyone
Who loves the sun

Who loves the rain
Who cares that it makes flowers
Who cares that it makes showers since you broke my heart
Who loves the sun
Who cares that it is shining
Who cares what it does since you broke my heart
Who loves the sun
Not everyone
Not just anyone
Who loves the sun

Sweet Jane (Final Version)

Standin' on the corner
Suitcase in my hand
Jack is in his corset, Jane is in her vest
And me, I'm in a rock 'n' roll band
Ridin' in a Stutz Bear Cat, Jim
You know those were different times
All the poets they studied rules of verse
And those ladies they rolled their eyes

Jack, he is a banker
And Jane, she is a clerk
And both of them save their monies
And when they come home from work
Sittin' down by the fire
The radio does play
A little classical music there, Jim
"The March of the Wooden Soldiers"
All you protest kids
You can hear Jack say

Some people they like to go out dancin'
And other peoples they have to work
And there's even some evil mothers
Well they're gonna tell you that everything is just dirt
You know that women never really faint
And that villians always blink their eyes
That children are the only ones who blush
And that life is just to die
But anyone who ever had a heart
They wouldn't turn around and break it
And anyone whoever played a part
They wouldn't turn around and hate it

Sweet Jane, sweet Jane

Rock 'n' Roll

Jenny said when she was just five years old
There was nothing happenin' at all
Every time she puts on a radio
There was nothin' goin' down at all
Then one fine mornin' she puts on a New York station
You know she don't believe what she heard at all
She started shakin' to that fine fine music
You know her life was saved by rock 'n' roll
Despite all the amputations you know you could just go out and
Dance to the rock 'n' roll station

Jenny said when she was just about five years old
You know my parents are gonna be the death of us all
Two TV sets and two Cadillac cars—
Ain't gonna help me at all
Then one fine mornin'
She turns on a New York station
She don't believe what she heard at all
She started dancin' to that fine fine music
You know her life was saved by rock 'n' roll
Despite all the computations
You could just dance to that rock 'n' roll station

And it was alright
It's alright now

Cool It Down

Somebody took the papers
And somebody's got the key
And somebody's nailed the door shut
And says, hey
Whatcha think that you see?
But me I'm down around the corner
You know I'm lookin for Miss Linda Lee
Because she's got the power to love me by the hour
Gives me W-L-O-V-E
If you want it so fast
Don't you know that it ain't gonna last
Of course you know it makes no difference to me

Somebody's got the time time
Somebody's got the right
All of the other people
Tryin' to use up the night
But now me, I'm out on the corner
You know I'm lookin' for Miss Linda Lee
Because she's got the power to love me by the hour
Gives me W-L-O-V-E
If you want it to last
Don't you know honey you can get it so fast
But of course
You know it makes no difference to me
You better cool it down

New Age (Final Version)

Can I have your autograph
He said to the fat blonde actress
You know I've seen every movie you've been in
From "Paths of Pain" to "Jewels of Glory"
And when you kissed Robert Mitchum
Gee, but I thought you'd never catch him

Over the hill right now
And you're looking for love
You're over the hill right now
And looking for love
I'll come runnin' to you
Honey when you want me
I'll come runnin' to you
Honey when you want me

Can I have your autograph
He said to the fat blonde actress
You know I know everything you've done
Anyway I hate divorces
To the left is a marble shower
It was fun even for an hour, but
You're over the hill right now
And lookin' for love
You're over the hill right now
And you're lookin' for love
I'll come runnin' to you
Honey when you want me
I'll come runnin' to you
Honey when you want me

Something's got a hold on me and I don't know what
Something's got a hold on me and I don't know what

It's the beginning of a new age

Head Held High

Momma told me
Ever since I was seven
Hold your head up high
My parents told me
Ever since I was eleven
Hold your head up high
They said the answer
Was to become a dancer
Hold your head up high
Oh just like I figured
They all was disfigured
With their head up high

Now I am older
I'm getting so much bolder
With my head up high
As I figured
Just like I figured
Set your heads up high
Just like I figured
You know they was disfigured
Hold your head high
You know they says the answer
Was to become a dancer
Hold your head up high boy

Ever since I was a baby
On my momma's knee
Oh just listening
To what everybody told me
But still the answer
Was to become a dancer
Hold your head up high
But just like I figured
They all was disfigured
Hold your heads up high

Lonesome Cowboy Bill

Lonesome Cowboy Bill rides the rodeo
Lonesome Cowboy Bill you gotta see him yodel-e-eo

Lonesome Cowboy Bill rides the rodeo
Ever since he was a little lad rode the rodeo
Buckin' broncs and sippin' wine
Got to see him go
And all the ten-gallon girls love to hear him yodel-e-eo
Lonesome Cowboy Bill rides the rodeo
Lonesome Cowboy Bill you gotta see him yodel-e-eo

Lonesome Cowboy Bill, still rides the rodeo
Up round Colorado shores, down by the Ohio
Sometimes even New Orleans down by Mardi Gras
And all the ten-gallon girls love to hear him yodel-e-eo
Lonesome Cowboy Bill rides the rodeo
Lonesome Cowboy Bill you gotta see him yodel-e-eo

You gotta to see him in the rodeo
When he's ridin' goin' too darn fast
You gotta to hear the people scream and shout
They call him Lonesome Cowboy Bill

I Found a Reason

I found a reason to keep living, and the reason dear is you
I found a reason to keep singing, and the reason dear is you
Oh, I do believe, if you don't like things you leave
For someplace you've never gone before

Honey, I found a reason to keep living
You know the reason dear it's you
I've walked down life's lonely highways
Hand in hand with myself
And I realize how many paths have crossed between us

Oh I do believe you are what you perceive
What comes is better than what came before

And you'd better come
Come come come to me
Come come come to me
You'd better come
Come come come to me

Train Round the Bend

Train round the bend
Takin' me away from the country
I'm sick of trees, take me to the city
Train goin' round the bend
Train comin' round the bend

Been in the country much too long
Trying to be a farmer
But nothing that I planted ever seemed to grow
Train comin' round the bend
Train comin' round the bend

I am just a city boy
I'm really not the country kind
I miss the city streets and the neon lights
See the train comin' round the bend
The train comin' round the bend

Once, she's goin' twice
She's gonna do it all up and down
She's goin' once, she's goin' twice
She's goin', train's comin' round the bend
You know the train's comin' round the bend

Hey, up and down, out of nowhere
Taking me back where I belong
I've been here once and I don't dig it tonight
The train's coming round the bend

Oh! Sweet Nothing

Say a word for Jimmy Brown, he ain't got nothing at all
Not the shirt right off his back, he ain't got nothing at all
Say a word for Ginger Brown
Walks with his head down to the ground
Took the shoes right off his feet
And threw the poor boy right out in the street
And this is what he said
Oh sweet nothing, she ain't got nothing at all
Oh sweet nothing, she ain't got nothing at all

Say a word for Pearly Mae
She can't tell the night from the day
They threw her out in the street
Just like a cat she landed on her feet

And say a word for Joanie Love
She ain't got nothing at all
Every day she falls in love
And every night she falls
And when she does she says
Oh sweet nothing, ain't got nothing at all
Oh sweet nothing, ain't got nothing at all

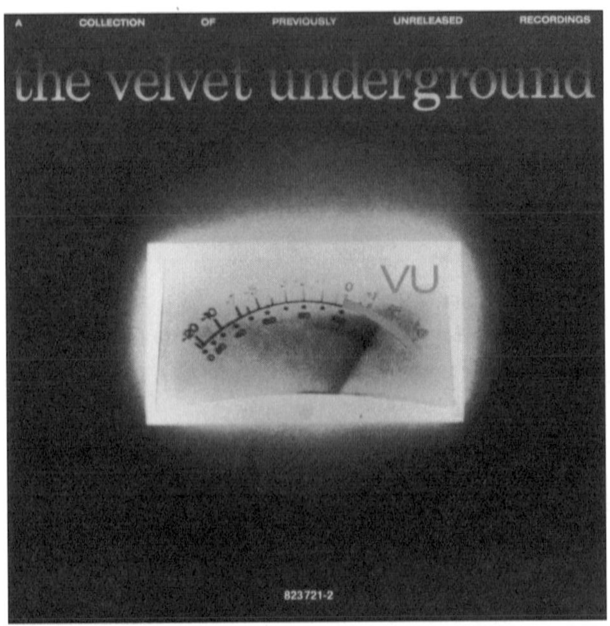
A COLLECTION OF PREVIOUSLY UNRELEASED RECORDINGS
the velvet underground
VU
823721-2

Stephanie Says

Stephanie says
That she wants to know
Why she's given half her life
To people she hates now

Stephanie says (Stephanie says)
When answering the phone (answering the phone)
What country shall I say is calling
From across the world

But she's not afraid to die
The people all call her Alaska
Between worlds, so the people ask her
'Cause it's all her mind
It's all in her mind

Stephanie says (Stephanie says)
That she wants to know (she wants to know)
Why it is, though she's the door
She can't leave the room

Stephanie says (Stephanie says)
But doesn't hang up the phone (hang up the phone)
What sea shell say is calling
From across the world

But she's not afraid to die
The people all call her Alaska
Between worlds, so the people ask her
'Cause it's all in her mind
It's all in her mind

They're asking is it good or bad
It's such an icy feeling
It's so cold in Alaska (Stephanie says)
It's so cold in Alaska (Stephanie says)
It's so cold in Alaska (Stephanie says)

Temptation Inside Your Heart

I know where temptation lies, inside of your heart
I know where the evil lies, inside of your heart
If you're gonna try to make it right
You're surely gonna end up wrong

I know where the mirror's edge is inside of your heart
I know where the razor's edge is inside of your heart
Well, if you're gonna make it right
You're surely gonna end up wrong
(Electricity comes from other planets)

I know where temptation lies, inside of your heart
I know where the evil lies, inside of your heart
Well, if you're gonna try to make it right
You're surely gonna end up wrong
(The Pope in the silver castle)

One of These Days

One of these days, ain't it peculiar
You're gonna look for me
And baby, I'll be gone

One of these days, and it won't be long
Oh darling, gonna call my name
And I'll be far gone

I'm gonna tell you something
That I ain't told no one before
That is iffn I can stop dancing
And get my poor self off this ballroom floor

One of these days, ain't it peculiar
Babe, you're gonna call my name
You know that I'll be gone, bye bye baby

I'm gonna tell you something
That I ain't told no one before
That is iffn I can stop dancing
And get my poor self off this ballroom floor

One of these days, and it won't be long
You're going to call my name
And I'll be gone
You're going to call my name
And I'll be gone
You're going to call my name child
And I'll be gone

I'm Sticking with You

I'm sticking with you
'Cause I'm made out of glue
Anything that you might do
I'm gonna do too

You held up a stagecoach in the rain
And I'm doing the same
Saw you hanging from a tree
And I made believe it was me

I'm sticking with you
'Cause I'm made out of glue
Anything that you might do
I'm gonna do, too

Moon people going to the stratosphere
Soldiers fighting with the Cong
But with you by my side I can do anything
When we swing, we hang past right and wrong

I'll do anything for you
Anything you'd want me to
I'll do anything for you
I'm sticking with you

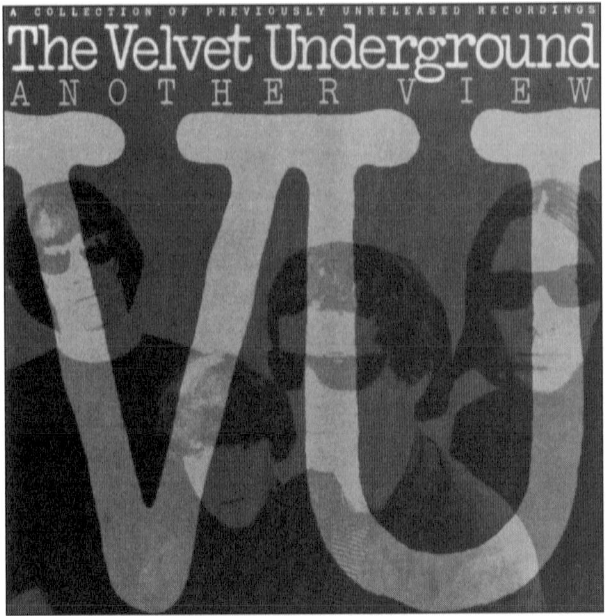
A COLLECTION OF PREVIOUSLY UNRELEASED RECORDINGS
The Velvet Underground
ANOTHER VIEW
VU

Hey Mr. Rain

Mr. Rain ain'tcha follow me down
Hey Mr. Rain ain'tcha follow me down
I been working baby oh so hard starin' up at the sky
Hey Mr. Rain ain'tcha follow me down

Mr. Rain ain'tcha gonna come down
Hey Mr. Rain ain'tcha gonna come down
I been working baby oh so hard staring up at the sky
Hey Mr. Rain gonna come down

Ferryboat Bill

Ferryboat Bill, won't you please come home?
You know your wife has married a midget's son
And that's the short and long of it

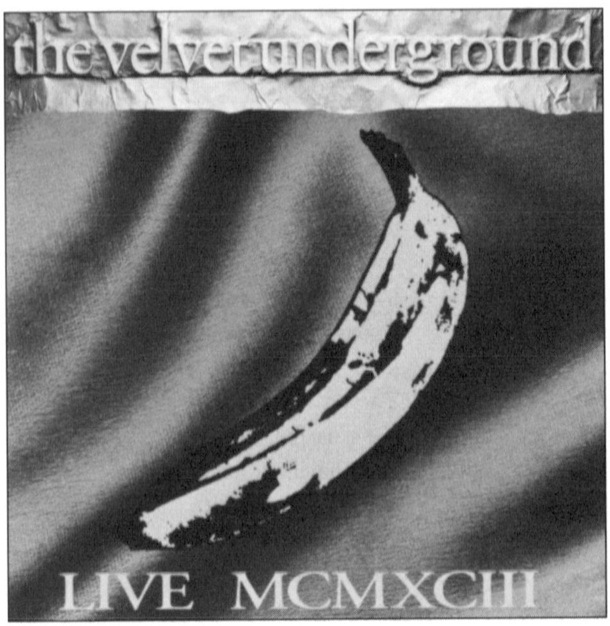
the velvet underground
LIVE MCMXCIII

Velvet Nursery Rhyme

We're the Velvet
Underground and we
have come to play /
It's been 28 years
since we've been
here to the day /
There's Maureen
she's on the drums
she's having a lotta
fun / Let's hear it
for Moe Tucker hit
those skins for
everyone / There is
Sterling Morrison
he's playing the
guitar / He's a gui-
tar hero kick their
asses really far

Now you got here
John and me / We
want no part of this
/ That's because we
think it is / Real
pretentious SHIT

Coyote

Coyote
goes to the top of the hill /
Doing the things that coyotes will /
Staring at the sky at the moon / You know he
starts to howl // Coyote goes to the mountaintop /
Looks over down at the river / says what a drop / No tame
dog is gonna take my bone // Coyote at the top of the hill /
Doing the things coyotes will / You gotta cast the first stone /
Cast the first stone // Jackal goes to the top of the hill / Doing the
things that jackals will / Staring at the moon / You know he starts to
howl // Wild dog up on a mountaintop / Blood in his jaws, the bone
he drops / No tame dog is ever ever gonna take my bone // Jackal up
on top of the hill / Doing the things that jackals will / Cast the first
stone / Cast the first stone // Coyote on top of the hill / Doing the
things that coyotes will / Staring at the sky he looks at the
moon he starts to howl // Coyote up on the mountaintop /
Blood in his jaws the bone he drops / Says no tame dog
is ever ever gonna take this bone // Coyote up on
a mountaintop / Says what a drop / You've
gotta cast the first stone / Cast
the first stone

NICO:
CHELSEA
GIRL

Chelsea Girls

Here's Room 506
It's enough to make you sick
Brigid's all wrapped up in foil
You wonder if she can uncoil
Here they come now
See them run now
Here they come now
Chelsea Girls

Here's Room 115
Filled with S&M queens
Magic marker row
You wonder just how high they go
Here's Pope dear Ondine
Rona's treated him so mean
She wants another scene
She wants to be a human being

Pepper she's having fun
She thinks she's some man's son
Her perfect loves don't last
Her future died in someone's past

Dear Ingrid's found her lick
She's turned another trick
Her treats and times revolve
She's got problems to be solved

Poor Mary, she's uptight she can't turn out her light
She rolled Susan in a ball
And now she can't see her at all

Dropout, she's in a fix
Amphetamine has made her sick
White powder in the air
She's got no bones and can't be scared

Here comes Johnny Bore
He collapsed on the floor
They shot him up with milk
And when he died, sold him for silk
Here they come now
See them run now
Here they come now
Chelsea Girls

Wrap Your Troubles in Dreams

Wrap your troubles in dreams
Send them all away
Put them in a bottle
And across the seas they'll stay

Speak not of misfortune
Speak not of your woes
Just steel yourself for holy death
Crouching by the door
Writhe and sway to music's pain
Searing with asides
Caress death with a lover's touch
For it shall be your bride

Slash the golden whip it snaps
'Cross the lovers' sides
The earth trembles without remorse

Preparing for to die
Salty ocean waves and sprays
Come crashing to the shore
Bullies kick and kill young loves
Down on barroom floors

Violence echoes through the land
And heart of every man
The knife stabs existent wounds
Pus runs through matted hair

The gleaming knife cuts early
Through the midnight air
Cutting entrails in its path
Blood runs without care

Excrement filters through the brain
Hatred bends the spine
Filth covers the body pores
To be cleansed by dying time

Wrap your troubles in dreams send them all away
Put them in a bottle
And across the seas they'll stay

LOU
REED

I Can't Stand It

It's hard being a man
Living in a garbage pail
My landlady called me up
She tried to hit me with a mop

I can't stand it any more more
But if Candy would just come back it'd be all right

I live with thirteen dead cats
A purple dog that wears spats
They're all out living in the hall
And I can't stand it anymore

I'm tired of living all alone
Nobody ever calls me on the phone
But when things start getting bad
I just play my music louder

I can't stand it any more more

Going Down

When you're in a dream
And you think you got your problems all nailed down
Pieces of the scheme seem to rattle up and then to rattle down
And when you start to fall
And those footsteps
They start to fade
Well, then you know you're going down
Yeah, you're falling all around
And you know you're going down for the last time

When you're in the air
And you're thinking
You'll drift off into the west
Your friend's polite, advise,
Hey, look you're pushing too hard
And perhaps you need a rest
And when you start to fall
And all those footsteps they start to fade
Then you know you're going down
Yeah, you're crashing upside down
And you know you're going down for the last

Time's not what it seems it just seems longer
When you're lonely in this world
Everything it seems
Would be brighter
If your nights were spent with some girl
Yeah, you're falling all around
Yeah, you're crashing upside down
And you know you're going down for the last time

Walk and Talk It

I got hearts in my looney tunes
I got dreams and you do, too
I got ten-wheel drive to pick you up, up to your ears
I got refined carbon in my eyelids, dear
I've got no one to love and no one to fear
You better walk it and talk it less you lose that beat

You better lose yourself mama
And knock yourself right off of your feet
You're moving too fast don't you want it to last
You better walk it talk it
You better walk it as you talk it less you lose that beat

I've got dimes in my shoes real nice
I've got bells that are laid on ice
I've got dreams, let me mix it with a little gin
I got cool when I'm cold and warm when I'm hot
But me is the one thing baby you ain't got
You got to walk it and talk it less you lose that beat

Lisa Says

Lisa says, on a night like this
It'd be so nice if you gave me a great big kiss
And Lisa says, hey honey, for just one little smile
I'll sing and play for you for the longest while

Lisa says, Lisa says
Lisa says, oh no Lisa says

Lisa says, honey, you must think I'm some kinda California fool
The way you treat me just like some kind of tool
Lisa says, hey baby, if you stick your tongue in my ear
Then the scene around here will become very clear

Lisa says, oh no Lisa says
Hey, don't you be a little baby
Lisa says, oh no Lisa says

Hey, if you're looking for a good time Charlie
Well, that's not really what I am
You know, some good time Charlie, always out having his fun
But if you're looking for some good good lovin'
Then sit yourself right over here
You know that those good, those good times
They just seem to pass me by just like pie in the sky
And Lisa says, on a night like this
It'd be so nice if you gave me a great big kiss
And Lisa says, hey baby, for just one little smile
I'll sing and play for you for the longest while

Why am I so shy
Why am I so shy
Jeez, you know that those good good times
They just seem to pass me by
Why am I so shy
First time I saw you, I was talking to myself
I says, hey you got those pretty, pretty eyes (such pretty eyes)
Now that you are next to me, I just get so upset
Hey Lisa, will you tell me, why am I so shy

Berlin

In Berlin, by the wall
You were five foot ten inches tall
It was very nice
Candlelight and Dubonnet on ice
We were in a small café
You could hear the guitars play
It was very nice
It was paradise

You're right and I'm wrong
You know I'm gonna miss you
Now that you're gone
One sweet day

In a small small café
We could hear the guitars play
It was very nice
Candlelight and Dubonnet on ice
Don't forget, hire a vet
He hasn't had that much fun yet
It was very nice
Hey honey, it was paradise

I Love You

When I think of all the things I've done
And I know that it's only just begun
Those smiling faces, you know I just can't forget 'em
But I love you

When I think of all the things I've seen
And I know that it's only the beginning
You know those smiling faces, I just can't forget 'em
But for now I love you

Just for a little while
Oh baby, just to see you smile
Just for a little while

When I think of all those things I've done
And I know that it's only just begun
Smiling smiling faces, Jesus, you know I can't forget them
But for now I love you
Right this minute, baby now, I love you
At least for now I love you

Wild Child

I was talking to Chuck in his Ghengis Khan suit
And his wizard's hat
He spoke of his movie and how he was making a new soundtrack
And then we spoke of kids on the coast
And different types of organic soap
And the way suicides don't leave notes
Then we spoke of Lorraine, always back to Lorraine

I was speaking to Bill
Who was given to pills and small racing cars
He had given them up since his last crack-up
Had carried him too far
Then we spoke of movies and verse and the way an actress held her purse
And the way life at times could get worse
Then we spoke of Lorraine, always back to Lorraine

I was talking to Betty about her auditions, how they made her ill
The life of the theater is certainly fraught
With many spills and chills
But she calmed down after some wine
Which is what happens most of the time
Then we sat and both spoke in rhyme
Till we spoke of Lorraine, ah, it's always back to Lorraine

I was talking to Ed who'd been reported dead by a mutual
friend
He thought it was funny that I had no money to spend on him
So we both shared a piece of sweet cheese
And sang of our lives and our dreams
And how things can come apart at the seams
And we talked of Lorraine, always back to Lorraine

She's a wild child and nobody can get at her
She's a wild child and nobody can get to her
Sleeping out on the street
Living all alone
Without a house or a home
And then she asks you please
Hey, baby can I have some spare change
Now can I break your heart?
She's a wild child, she's a wild child

Love Makes You Feel

Life isn't what it seems
I'm forever drifting into dreams
Such a sad affair
To always be drifting into air

But it's not what you say or you do
That makes me feel like I am falling
It's things that we've both been through
That makes me feel like I am upside down
And love makes you feel ten foot tall
Yes, love makes you feel ten foot tall

Just a funny thing
I'm forever drifting into dreams
Just not the proper thing
To always be drifting into dreams

But it's not what you say or do
That makes me feel like I am falling
It's things that we've both been through
That makes me feel like I am upside down
And love makes you feel ten foot tall
Yes, love makes you feel ten foot tall

And it sounds like this

Ride Into the Sun

Looking for another chance
For someone else to be
Looking for another place
To ride into the sun

Ride into the sun
Ride into the sun
Ride into the sun
Ride into the sun

The sun
Where everything seems so pretty
But if you're tired and you're sick of the city
Remember that it's just a flower made out of clay

The City
Where everything seems so dirty
But if you're tired and you're filled with self-pity
Remember that you're just one more person who's there

It's hard to live in the city

Ocean

Here comes the ocean and the waves down by the sea
Here comes the ocean and the waves where have they been

Don't swim tonight my love
The sea is mad my love
It's known to drive men crazy

Malcolm has burned at sea
The castle it sits and reeks
The madness can make you hazy

But here comes the waves
Down by the shore
Washing the rocks that have been here centuries or more
Down by the sea

Here comes the ocean and the waves down by the sea
Here comes the ocean and the waves where have they been

Castles glowing at night
Towers above our fright
Warlocks decapitating
Malcolm he lives on hate
Serves your brain on a plate
Feasts on your mouth for dinner

But here comes the waves down by the sea
Washing the eyes of the men who have died
Down by the sea

LOU REED-TRANSFORMER

Vicious

Vicious, you hit me with a flower
You do it every hour
Oh baby, you're so vicious
Vicious, you want me to hit you with a stick
But all I've got's a guitar pick
Baby, you're so vicious

When I watch you come, baby I just wanna run far away
You're not the kind of person 'round I wanna stay
When I see you walkin' down the street
I step on your hands and I mangle your feet
You're not the kind of person that I want to meet
Babe, you're so vicious, you're just so vicious

Vicious, you hit me with a flower
You do it every hour
Oh baby, you're so vicious

Vicious, Hey! Why don't you swallow razor blades
You must think that I'm some kind of gay blade
But baby, you're so vicious

When I see you comin' I just have to run
You're not good and you certainly aren't very much fun

When I see you walkin' down the street
I step on your hand and I mangle your feet
You're not the kind of person that I even want to meet
'Cause you're so vicious

Andy's Chest

If I could be anything in the world that flew
I would be a bat and come swooping after you
And if the last time you were here things were a bit askew
Well, you know what happens after dark
When rattlesnakes lose their skins and their hearts
And all the missionaries lose their bark
Oh, all the trees are calling after you
And all the venom snipers after you
Are all the mountains bolder after you?

If I could be any one of the things in this world that bite
Instead of an indentured ocelot on a leash, I'd rather be a kite
And be tied to the end of your string
And flying in the air, babe, at night
'Cause you know what they say about honey bears
When you shave off all their baby hair
You have a hairy-minded pink bare bear

And all the bells are rolling out for you
And stones are all erupting out for you
And all the cheap bloodsuckers are flying after you

Yesterday, Daisy May and Biff were grooving on the street
And just like in a movie her hands became her feet
Her belly button was her mouth
Which meant she tasted what she'd speak

But the funny thing is what happened to her nose
It grew until it reached all of her toes
Now when people say her feet smell they mean her nose

And curtains laced with diamonds dear for you
And all the Roman noblemen for you
And kingdom's Christian soldiers dear for you
And melting ice cap mountain tops for you
And knights in flaming silver robes for you
And bats that with a kiss turn prince for you
Swoop Swoop
Rock Rock

Perfect Day

Just a perfect day
Drink sangria in the park
And then later when it gets dark
We go home

Just a perfect day
Feed animals in the zoo
Then later a movie too
And then home

Oh it's such a perfect day
I'm glad I spent it with you
Oh such a perfect day
You just keep me hangin' on
You just keep me hangin' on

Just a perfect day, problems all left alone
Weekenders on our own, it's such fun
Just a perfect day, you made me forget myself
I thought I was someone else, someone good

You're going to reap just what you sow

Hangin' Round

Harry was a rich young man, who would become a priest
He dug up his dear father, who was recently deceased
He did it with tarot cards and a mystically attuned mind
And shortly there and after he did find

Jeanie was a spoiled young brat, she thought she knew it all
She smoked mentholated cigarettes and she had sex in the hall
But she was not my kind, or even of my sign
The kind of animal that I would be about

You keep hangin' round me and
I'm not so glad you found me
You're still doing things that I gave up years ago
You keep hangin' round me and
I'm not so glad you found me
You're still doing things that I gave up years ago

Kathy was a bit surreal, she painted all her toes
And on her face she wore dentures, clamped tightly to her nose
And when she finally spoke, her twang her glasses broke
And no one else could smoke while she was in the room

Hark, the herald angels sang and reached out for a phone
And plucking it with a knife in hand dialed long distance home
But it was all too much, sprinkling angel dust
To AT&T who didn't wish you well

You keep hangin' round me and
I'm not so glad you found me
You're still doing things that I gave up years ago
You keep hangin' round me and
I'm not so glad you found me
You're still doing things that I gave up years ago

Hangin' round, that's all you're doing baby
Hangin' round

Walk on the Wild Side

Holly came from Miami F-L-A
Hitchhiked her way across the U.S.A
Plucked her eyebrows on the way
Shaved her legs and then he was a she
She says, Hey babe, take a walk on the wild side
Said, Hey honey, take a walk on the wild side

Candy came from out on the Island
In the backroom she was everybody's darling
But she never lost her head even when she was givin'
head
She says, Hey babe, take a walk on the wild side
Said, Hey babe, take a walk on the wild side
And the colored girls go
Doo da doo da doo
Doo da doo
Doo da doo da doo
Doo da doo
Doo da doo da doo
Doo da doo
Doo

Little Joe never once gave it away
Everybody had to pay and pay
A hustle here and a hustle there
New York City is the place where they said
Hey babe, take a walk on the wild side
I said, Hey Joe, take a walk on the wild side

Sugar Plum Fairy came and hit the streets
Lookin' for soul food and a place to eat
Went to the Apollo
You should've seen 'im go go go
They said, Hey Sugar, take a walk on the wild side
I said, Hey babe, take a walk on the wild side

Jackie is just speeding away
Thought she was James Dean for a day
Then I guess she had to crash
Valium would have helped that bash
She said, Hey babe, take a walk on the wild side
I said, Hey honey, take a walk on the wild side

Make Up

Your face when sleeping is sublime
And then you open up your eyes
Then comes pancake factor number one
Eyeliner rose hips and lip gloss such fun
You're a slick little girl
You're a slick little girl

Rouge and coloring, incense and ice
Perfume and kisses ooh it's all so nice
You're a slick little girl
You're such a slick little girl

Now we're coming out
Out of our closets
Out on the streets
Yeah we're coming out

When you're in bed it's so wonderful
It'd be so nice to fall in love
When you get dressed I really get my fill
People say that it's impossible

Gowns lovely made out of lace
And all the things that you do to your face
You're a slick little girl, oh you're a slick little girl

Eyeliner whitener then color the eyes
Yellow and green ooh what a surprise
You're a slick little girl, oh, you're such a slick little girl
Now we're coming out
Out of our closets
Out on the streets
Yes, we're coming out

Satellite of Love

Satellite's gone up to the skies
Things like that drive me out of my mind
I watched it for a little while
I like to watch things on TV

Satellite of love

Satellite's gone way up to Mars
Soon it'll be filled with parking cars
I watched it for a little while
I love to watch things on TV

I've been told that you've been bold
With Harry, Mark and John
Monday and Tuesday
Wednesday through Thursday
With Harry, Mark and John

Satellite's gone up to the skies
Things like that drive me out of my mind
I watched it for a little while
I love to watch things on TV

Satellite of love

Wagon Wheel

Won'tcha be my wagon wheel (spoke spoke)
Won'tcha tell me baby how does it feel?
You've gotta live yeah your life as though you're number one
Yeah, you've gotta live yeah your life
And make a point of having some fun
But iff'n you think that you get kicks from flirting with danger
Just kick her in the head and rearrange her

Oh heavenly father what can I do
What she's done to me is making me crazy
Oh heavenly father I know I have sinned
But look where I've been
It's making me lazy

Why don't you wake me, shake me
(Please) Don't let me sleep too long

New York Telephone Conversation

I was sleeping gently napping when I heard the phone
Who is on the other end talking
Am I even home
Did you see what she did to him
Did you hear what they said
Just a New York conversation rattling in my head

Oh oh my, and what shall we wear
Oh oh my, and who really cares

Just a New York conversation
Gossip all of the time
Did you hear who did what to whom
Happens all the time
Who has touched and who has dabbled
Here in the city of shows
Openings, closings, bad repartee
Everybody knows

Oh how sad, and why do we call
Oh I'm glad, to hear from you all

I am calling
Yes I'm calling
Just to speak to you
For I know this night will kill me
If I can't be with you
If-I-can't-be-with-you

I'm So Free

Yes, I am Mother Nature's son
And I'm the only one
I do what I want and I want what I see
Could only happen to me

I'm so free
I'm so free

Oh please, Saint Germaine
I have come this way
Do you remember the shape I was in
I had horns and fins

I'm so free
I'm so free
Do you remember the silver walks
You used to shiver and I used to talk
Then we went down to Times Square
And ever since, I've been hangin' round there

I'm so free
I'm so free

Goodnight Ladies

Goodnight ladies, ladies goodnight
It's time to say goodbye
Let me tell you now
Goodnight ladies, ladies goodnight
It's time to say goodbye

Now all night long you've been drinking your tequila
But now you've sucked your lemon peel dry
So why not get high, high, high and
Goodnight ladies, ladies goodnight

Goodnight ladies, ladies goodnight
It's time to say goodbye
Goodnight sweet ladies, ladies goodnight
It's time to say goodbye, bye, bye

We've been together for the longest time
But now it's time to get high
Come on let's get high, high, high
And goodnight ladies, ladies goodnight

Oh I'm still missing my other half
It must be something I did in the past
Don't it just make you wanna laugh
It's a lonely Saturday night

Nobody calls me on the telephone
I put another record on my stereo
But I'm still singing a song of you
It's a lonely Saturday night

Now if I was an actor or a dancer who was glamorous
Then you know an amorous life would soon be mine
But now the tinsel light of starbreak
Is all that's left to applaud my heartbreak
And at 11 o'clock I watch the network news

Something tells me that you're really gone
You said we could be friends but that's not what I want
Anyway, my TV dinner's almost done
It's a lonely Saturday night

LOU REED
BERLIN

Lady Day

When she walked on down the street
She was like a child staring at her feet
But when she passed the bar
And she heard the music play
She had to go in and sing
It had to be that way
She had to go in and sing
It had to be that way

After the applause had died down
And the people drifted away
She climbed down off the bar
And went out the door
To the hotel
That she called home
It had greenish walls
A bathroom in the hall
And I said no, no, no,
Oh, Lady Day
I said no, no, no,
Oh, Lady Day

Men of Good Fortune

Men of good fortune, often cause empires to fall
While men of poor beginnings, often can't do anything at all
The rich son waits for his father to die
The poor just drink and cry
And me, I just don't care at all

Men of good fortune, very often can't do a thing
While men of poor beginnings, often can do anything
At heart they try to act like a man
Handle things the best way they can
They have no rich daddy to fall back on

Men of good fortune, often cause empires to fall
While men of poor beginnings often can't do anything at all
It takes money to make money they say
Look at the Fords, didn't they start that way
Anyway, it makes no difference to me

Men of good fortune, often wish that they could die
While men of poor beginnings want what *they* have
And to get it they'll die

All those great things that life has to give
They wanna have money and live
But me, I just don't care at all
About men of good fortune, men of poor beginnings

Caroline Says I

Caroline says that I'm just a toy
She wants a man not just a boy
Oh Caroline says, ooh Caroline says

Caroline says she can't help but be mean
Or cruel, or oh so it seems
Oh Caroline says, Caroline says

She says she doesn't want a man who leans
Still she is my Germanic Queen
Yeah, she's my Queen

The things she does, the things she says
People shouldn't treat others that way
But at first I thought I could take it all
Just like poison in a vial, hey she was often very vile
But of course, I thought I could take it all

Caroline says that I'm not a man
So she'll go get it catch as catch can
Oh Caroline says, yeah Caroline says

Caroline says moments in time
Can't continue to be only mine
Oh Caroline says, yeah Caroline says

She treats me like I am a fool
But to me she's still a German Queen
Ooh, she's my Queen

How Do You Think It Feels

How do you think it feels
When you're speeding and lonely
How do you think it feels
When all you can say is if only
If only I had a little
If only I had some change
If only, if only, only
How do you think it feels
And when do you think it stops

How do you think it feels
When you've been up for five days
Hunting around always, 'cause you're afraid of sleeping

How do you think it feels
To feel like a wolf and foxy
How do you think it feels
To always make love by proxy

How do you think it feels
And when do you think it stops!
When do you think it stops

Oh, Jim

All your two-bit friends they're shootin' you up with pills
They said that it was good for you, that it would cure your ills
I don't care just where it's at, I'm just like an alley cat
And when you're filled up to here with hate
Don't you know you gotta get it straight
Filled up to here with hate
Beat her black and blue and get it straight
Do, do, do, do, do, do

When you're lookin' through the eyes of hate
All your two-bit friends, they asked you for your autograph
They put you on the stage, they thought it'd be good for a laugh
But I don't care just where it's at
'Cause honey I'm just like an alley cat

And when you're filled up to here with hate
Don't you know you gotta get it straight—
Filled up to here with hate
Beat her black and blue and get it straight

Oh Jim, how could you treat me this way
Hey hey hey, how'd you treat me this way
Oh Jim, how could you treat me this way
Hey hey, how'd you treat me this way
You know you broke my heart ever since you went away

Now you said that you loved us
But you only made love to one of us
Oh oh oh oh Jim, how could you treat me this way
You know you broke my heart ever since you went away

When you're looking through the eyes of hate oh whoa whoa whoa
When you're looking through the eyes of hate oh whoa whoa whoa
When you're looking through the eyes of hate

Caroline Says II

Caroline says, as she gets up off the floor
Why is it that you beat me, it isn't any fun
Caroline says, as she makes up her eye
You ought to learn more about yourself, think more than just I

But she's not afraid to die
All of her friends call her Alaska
When she takes speed, they laugh and ask her
What is in her mind
What is in her mind

Caroline says, as she gets up from the floor
You can hit me all you want to, but I don't love you anymore
Caroline says, while biting her lip
Life is meant to be more than this and this is a bum trip

She put her fist through the window pane
It was such a funny feeling

It's so cold in Alaska

The Kids

They're taking her children away
Because they said she was not a good mother
They're taking her children away
Because she was making it with sisters and brothers
And everyone else, all of the others
Like cheap officers who would stand there and
Flirt in front of me

They're taking her children away
Because they said she was not a good mother
They're taking her children away
Because of the things that they heard she had done
The black Air Force sergeant was not the first one
And all of the drugs she took, every one, every one

And I am the Water Boy
The real game's not over here
But my heart is overflowing anyway
I'm just a tired man, no words to say
But since she lost her daughter
It's her eyes that fill with water
And I am much happier this way

They're taking her children away
Because they said she was not a good mother

They're taking her children away
Because number one was the girlfriend from Paris
The things that they did they didn't have to ask us
And then the Welshman from India, who came here to stay

They're taking her children away
Because they said she was not a good mother
They're taking her children away
Because of the things she did in the streets
In the alleys and bars, no she couldn't be beat
That miserable rotten slut couldn't turn anyone away

The Bed

This is the place where she lay her head
When she went to bed at night
And this is the place our children were conceived
Candles lit the room at night

And this is the place where she cut her wrists
That odd and fateful night
And I said, oh, oh, oh, oh, oh what a feeling

This is the place where we used to live
I paid for it with love and blood
And these are the boxes that she kept on the shelf
Filled with her poetry and stuff
And this is the room where she took the razor
And cut her wrists that strange and fateful night

I never would have started if I'd known
That it'd end this way
But funny thing I'm not at all sad
That it stopped this way

This is the place where she lay her head
When she went to bed at night
And this is the place our children were conceived
Candles lit the room brightly at night
And this is the place where she cut her wrists
That odd and fateful night
And I said, oh, oh, oh, oh, oh, oh, oh what a feeling

Sad Song

Staring at my picture book
She looks like Mary, Queen of Scots
She seemed very regal to me
Just goes to show you how wrong you can be
I'm gonna stop wasting my time
Somebody else would have broken both of her arms
Sad song

My castle, kids and home
I thought she was Mary, Queen of Scots
I tried so very hard
Shows just how wrong you can be

I'm gonna stop wasting my time
Somebody else would have broken both of her arms

LOU REED
SALLY
CAN'T DANCE

Ride Sally Ride

Sit yourself down
Bang out a tune on that grand piano
Sit yourself down
Lay languidly down upon the sofa
Oohh isn't it nice, when your heart is made out of ice

Ride Sally Ride
It's not your time, or way of confusion
Ride Sally Ride
'Cause if you don't, you'll get a contusion
Oohh isn't it nice, when you find your heart's made out of ice

Sit yourself down, take off your pants
Don't you know this is a party
Sit yourself down, why do you think
We brought all these people, Miss Brandy?

Animal Language

Miss Riley had a dog, she used to keep it in her back yard
And when the dog began to bark
All the neighbors began to shout
Then came a stormy night, Miss Riley let her dog out
And when the neighbors found him round
They put a gun down his mouth and shot him down

He went oohh wow bow wow oohh wow bow wow

Miss Murphy had a cat, on her lap it sat
And once in a great big while
It looked like that Cheshire Cat did smile
But often it used to chase, anything that crossed its face
But one day it got so hot that Cheshire Cat had a blood clot

And she said oohh yow meow meow
Oohh yow me meow

Then the dog met the cat, the dog was hot and the cat was wet
Then in came some sweaty dude, he put a board between the two
Then they couldn't get at it, got frustrated all about it
So they did the only thing you could do
They took the dude's sweat, and shot it up between the two

They said oohh wow bow wow, oohh wow meow

Baby Face

Jim, living with you's not such fun, you're not the only one
You don't have the looks
You're not the person that you used to be
And there are people on the street that would go for me
And I said no, no, no, no, no Baby Face

I met you in a bar in L.A., I was not feeling so good
You did the proper moves, you did everything that you should
But now you're making a mistake
And somebody else will take your place
You're taking drugs over me
And I said no, no, no, no, no Baby Face

You're not the kind of person it's easy to live with in a house
I cook all your meals, I make sure that you work out
But lately it's been gettin' so hard, the way you talk
(Man you don't split your stash or your bread)
The way you walk
(You can keep it)
And I'm not sure exactly what it's all about
And I said no, no, no, no, no Baby Face
(You can keep it just keep it)

N.Y. Stars

The stock is empty in our eyeball store
All we got left a few cataracts and sores
The faggot mimic machine never had ideas
Mission impossible they self-destruct on fear

On a standard New York night
Ghouls go to see their so-called stars
A fairly stupid thing
To pay five bucks for fourth-rate imitators

They say:
"I'm so empty
No surface, no depth
Oh please can't I be you
Your personality's so great"

Like new buildings
Square, tall and the same
Sorry Ms. Stupid
Didn't know you didn't know it's a game
I'm just waitin' for them to hurry up and die
It's really getting too crowded here
Help your New York Stars

Contributions accepted all the same
We need a new people store
Remember we're very good at games

Kill Your Sons

All your two bit psychiatrists are giving you electric shock
They said they'd let you live at home with mom and dad
Instead of mental hospitals
But every time you tried to read a book you couldn't
Get to page seventeen
'Cause you forgot where you were
So you couldn't even read

Mom informed me on the phone she didn't know what to do about dad
He took an axe and broke the table aren't you glad you're married
And sister she got married on the Island
And her husband takes the train
He's big and he's fat—and he doesn't have a brain

Creedmore treated me very good
But Payne Whitney was even better
And when I flipped out on PHC
I was so sad—I didn't even get a letter

All of the drugs that we took, it really was a lot of fun
But when they shoot you up with thorazine on crystal smoke
You choke like a son of a gun

Don't you know?
They're gonna kill your sons
Until they run run run run run run run run away

Ennui

All the things you said, you thought I was dead
Everything made me feel aware
Ah, you're getting old, you're doing things
You're losing your hair
All of the things that you used to believe in
Turned out to be true
You're guilty of reason

You're the kind of person that I could do without
Certain kinds of money
Would make you see what it's all about
There's a first time for everything
And the first one's on me
Don't you see

All of the things that your old lover said
Well look at them, they jump out of windows
And now they're just dead
It's the truth, don't you realize

They live without any talent or fun
Running out on the streets
Balling anyone
It's the truth
It's the truth

Pick up the pieces that make up your life
Maybe someday you'll have a wife
And then alimony
Oh, can't you see

Sally Can't Dance

Sally dances on the floor
She says that she can't do it anymore
She walks down Saint Mark's Place
And eats natural food at my place

Now, Sally can't dance no more
She can't get it off of the floor
Sally can't dance no more
They've got her in the trunk of a Ford
She can't dance no more

Sally is losing her face
She lives on Saint Mark's Place
In a rent-controlled apartment, eighty dollars a month
She has lots of fun, she has lots of fun, but

Sally can't dance no more
Sally can't dance no more
She took too much meth, and can't get off of the floor
Now Sally, she can't dance no more

She was the first girl in the neighborhood
To wear tie-dyed pants
A-like-a-she should
She was the first girl that I ever seen
That had flowers painted on her jeans
She was the first girl in her neighborhood
Who got raped in Tompkins Square
Real good
Now, she wears a sword like Napoleon
And she kills the boys and acts like a son

Watch this now
Sally became a big model
She moved up to Eightieth and Park
She had a studio apartment
And that's where she used to ball folk singers

Sally can't dance no more
Sally can't dance no more
Sally can't get herself off the floor
Sally can't dance no more

She knew all the really right people
She went to Les Jardin
She danced with Picasso's illegitimate mistress and wore
Kenneth Lane jewelry—it's trash, But

Sally can't dance no more

Billy

Billy was a good friend of mine
We grew up together ever since we were nine
We went to school he was my best friend
And I thought our friendship would never end

In high school he played football
And me I didn't do anything at all
He made touchdowns while I played pool
And no one could figure out which one of us was the fool

Then we both went off to college
He studied medicine while I studied foliage
He got A's, I got D's
He was going for his Ph.D.

Then I decided to drop out
Things were getting a little too hot
Billy stayed then became an intern then a doctor

Then war broke out and he had to go
But not me I was mentally unfit or so or so they say so-so

When he came back he wasn't quite the same
His nerves were shot but not me
Last time I saw him I couldn't take it anymore
He wasn't the Billy I knew
It was like talking to a door

Billy was a friend of mine
I grew up with him ever since I was nine
We went together through school
Now I often wonder which one of us was the fool

Lou Reed
METAL MACHINE MUSIC
AN ELECTRONIC INSTRUMENTAL COMPOSITION
*THE AMINE β RING
*dextrorotory components
synthesis of
sympathomimetic musics

Liner Notes

Passion--REALISM--realism was the key. The records were letters. Real letters from me to certain other people. Who had and still have basically, no music, be it verbal or instrumental, to listen to. One of the peripheral effects, typically distorted, was what was to be known as heavy metal rock. In Reality it was of course diffuse, obtuse, weak, boring and ultimately an embarrassment. This record is not for parties/ dancing/ background, romance. This is what I meant by "real" rock, about "real" things. No one I know has listened to it all the way through including myself. It is not meant to be. Start any place you like. Symmetry, mathematical precision, obsessive and detailed accuracy and the vast advantage one has over "modern electronic composers." They, with neither sense of time, melody or emotion, manipulated or no. It's for a certain time and place of mind. It is the only recorded work I know of seriously done as well as possible as a gift, if one could call it that, from a part of certain head, to a few others. Most of you won't like this, and I don't blame you at all. It's not meant for you. At the very least I made it so I had something to listen to. Certainly Misunderstood: Power to Consume (how Bathetic); an idea done respectfully, intelligently, sympathetically and graciously, always with concentration on the first and foremost goal. For that matter, off the record, I love and adore it. I'm sorry, but not especially, if it turns you off.

One record for us and it. I'd harbored hope that the intelligence that once inhabited novels or films would ingest rock. I was, perhaps, wrong. This is the reason *Sally Can't Dance*--your *Rock n Roll Animal*. More than a decent try, but hard for us to do badly. Wrong media, unquestionably. This is not meant for the market. The agreement one makes with "speed." A specific acknowledgment. A to say the least, very limited market. *Rock n Roll Animal* makes this possible, funnily enough. The misrepresentation succeeds to the point of making possible the appearance of the progenitor. For those for whom the needle is no more than a toothbrush. Professionals, no sniffers please, don't confuse superiority (no competition) with violence, power or other justifications. The Tacit speed agreement with Self. We did not start World War I, II, or III. Or the Bay of Pigs, for that Matter. Whenever. As way of disclaimer, I am forced to say that, due to stimulation of various centers (remember OOOHHHMMM, etc.), the possible negative contraindications must be pointed out. A record has to, of all things Anyway, hypertense people, etc. possibility of epilepsy (petite mal), psychic motor disorders, etc., etc., etc. My week beats your year.

Lou Reed

Liner Notes

[illegible] REALISM [illegible]

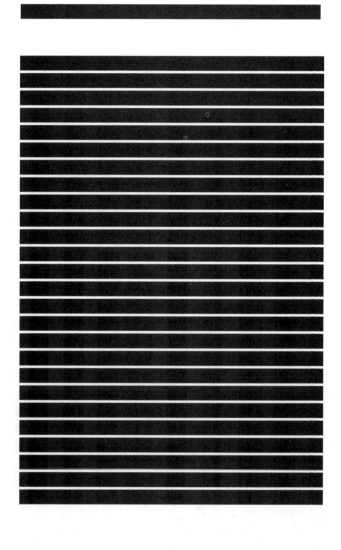

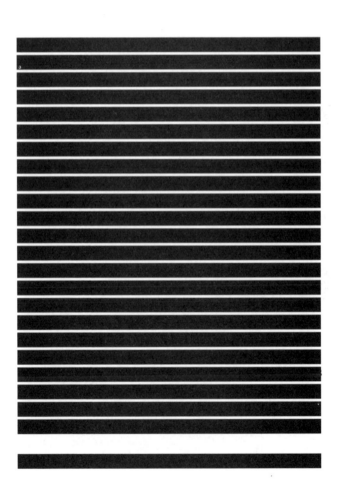

CONEY ISLAND
BABY

Crazy Feeling

You're the kind of person that I've been dreaming of
You're the kind of person that I always wanted to love
And when I first seen you walk right through that bar door
And I seen those suit-and-tie Johns buy you one drink
Then buy you some more

I had—I knew you had that crazy feeling
Now you've got that crazy feelin'
You know I've had that crazy feeling, too
I can see it in ya

Now everybody knows that business ends at three
And everybody knows an after-hours love is free
And you, you really are a queen ah such a queen, such a queen
And I know 'cause I've made the same scene
I know just what you mean because

You've got that crazy feelin' now now now
You've got that that crazy feelin'
You've got that crazy feelin' deep inside
Now I can see it in your eyes

I feel just like, feel just like ya

Charley's Girl

Everybody said that you better watch out
Man, she's gonna turn you in
And me, you know that I thought I lucked out
And now look at the trouble that I'm in
You better watch out for Charley's girl

It happened on New Year's Eve
They said everybody had to leave
They had a warrant in their hand
They wanted to bust the whole band
I said if I ever see Sharon again
I'm gonna punch her face in
Watch out for Charley's girl
You know she'll turn you in

She's My Best Friend

She's my best friend, certainly not your average girl
She's my best friend
She understands me when I'm feeling down, down, down,
  down, down, down
You know it sure hurts to be that way
Down, down, down, down, down, down
You know that it sure hurts to know that you're that kinda fellow

Here's to Mulberry Jane
She made Jim when she came
Somebody cut off her feet, now Jelly rolls in the street

If you want to see me, well honey, you know that I'm not around
But if you want to hear me why don'tcha just turn around
I'm by the window where the light is

She's my best friend
Certainly not just like your average dog or car
She's my best friend
She understands me when I'm feeling down, down, down, down,
down, down
You know it sure hurts to be that way
Down, down, down, down, down, down
You know it sure hurts to know that you're that kinda fellow

Let's hear one for Newspaper Joe
He caught his hand in the door
Dropped his teeth on the floor
They said, "Hey now Joe, guess that's the way the news goes"

If you want to see, see me, well baby, you know that I'm not around
But if you want to feel, feel me why don'tcha just turn around
I'm by the window where the light is

Kicks

Hey man, what's your style
How you get your kicks for livin'
Hey man, what's your style
How you get your adrenaline flowin' now

Hey man, what's your style
I love the way you drive your car now
Hey man, what's your style
I ain't jealous of the way you're livin'

When you cut that dude with that stiletto, man, you
You did it so, ah, cheaply
When the blood come-a-down his neck
Don't you know it was a better than sex
Now, now, now
It was-a-way-a better than gettin' laid—'cause it's the
Final thing to do now
Get somebody to, uh, come on to you
Then you just
Get somebody to now now come on to you and then
You kill them,
You kill them

'Cause I need kicks
Hey baby, babe I need kicks, now
I'm gettin' bored, I need a need a need a now now now
some kicks
Oh give it give it give it now now some kicks
When you stabbed that cat with that knife
You did it so, ah, crudely, now

When the blood came down his chest-uh
It was way better than a sex
It was way better than getting' A it was a
The final thing to do

A Gift

I'm just a gift to the women of this world
I'm just a gift to the women of this world
Responsibility sits so ah hard on my shoulder
Like a good wine, I'm better as I grow older
And now, I'm just a gift to the women of this world

I'm just a gift to the women of this world
I'm just a gift to the women of this world

It's hard to settle for second best
After you've had me, you know that you've had the best
And now you know that I'm just a gift to women of this world

Just a gift, now

Ooohhh Baby

You're the kind of girl
That everybody's wondering about
You're the kind of person
That everybody's a-staring at
But now you're a topless dancer
Working out of a bar on Times Square
And everybody wishes you were back
In the massage parlor back there on Ninth Avenue (311)
You make me go
Ooh baby, Ooh baby, Ooh baby ooh ooh ooh
Ooh baby, Ooh baby, Ooh baby ooh ooh ooh

Your old man was the best B and E man
Down on the streets
And all the guys on the precinct
Always was watching for him on their beat
But when he ripped off Seymour
He was really not a-doing so fine
And everything is not swelled 'cept his hands and legs
And maybe even mine

He's feeling maybe it's good that they said
Ooh baby, Ooh baby, Ooh baby ooh
Ooh baby, Ooh baby, Ooh hey babe, ooh ooh ooh

It's very funny asking me
Why they keep the lights on down so low
Well, yesterday's trade's today's competition
Or didn't you know
And all florescent lighting makes it
So your wrinkles, they don't show
And it's very funny, the way your
Twenty bucks an hour, can a-go
If you don't make me go now now now
Ooh baby, Ooh baby, Ooh ooh baby ooh
Ooh baby, Ooh baby, Ooh baby ooh ooh ooh

Everybody wondered about you
When you were seen in drinking some beer
You got here from Ohio and your mother said
You'd book her and be real near
That's the way it goes now
Ooh baby, Ooh baby, Ooh baby ooh ooh ooh
Hey shake your buns now, mama
Walk it now, get down

Nobody's Business

Hey, if you're moving too fast
Don't you want this thing to last
But if you start moving slow
Then hey pretty mama, you just will have to go, because
It's nobody's business but my own
No no no no no, no no no no no

But if you start acting mean
Then I'll have to mess up the scene
But if you start treating me nice
Hey now baby I'm gonna have to raise your price, because
It's nobody's business but my own

Coney Island Baby

You know when I was a young man in high school
You believe it or not
I wanted to play football for the coach
And all those older guys,
They said that he was mean and cruel,
But you know, I wanted to play for the coach

They said I was a little too light weight
To play line backer
So's I'm playing right end
I want to play football for the coach
'Cause you know someday man you got to stand up straight
Unless you're gonna fall
And then you're goin' to die
And the straightest dude I ever knew
Was standing right by me all the time
So I had to play football for the coach
Man I wanted to play football for the coach

When you're all alone and lonely in your midnight hour
And you find that your soul, it's been up for sale
And you begin to think about all the things that you've done
And begin to hate just about everything
But remember the princess who lived on the hill,
Who loved you even though she knew you was wrong
And right now she just might come shining throug

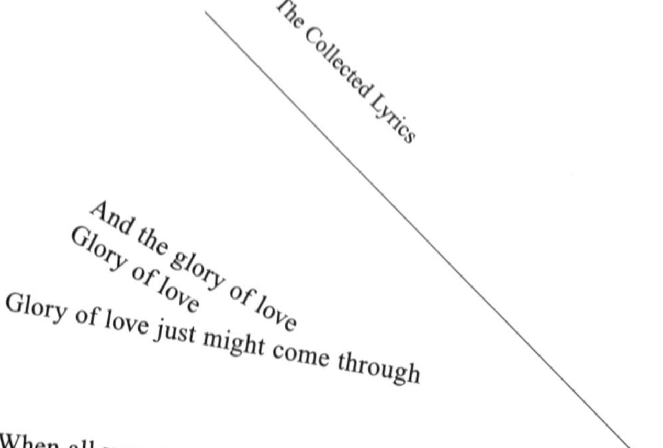

And the glory of love
Glory of love
Glory of love just might come through

When all your two-bit friends have gone and ripped you off
And they're talkin' behind your back sayin' man you are never
Gonna be no human being
Then you start thinkin' again about all those things that you done
And who it was and what it was
And all the different things
You made every different scene

But remember that the city is a funny place
Something like a circus or a sewer
And just remember different people have peculiar tastes

And the glory of love
The glory of love
The glory of love
Might see you through

I'm a Coney Island Baby now

I'd like to send this one out to Lou and Rachel and
all the kids in PS 192

Man I swear I'd give the whole thing up for you

Rock and Roll Heart

I Believe in Love

I believe in good times now
And I believe in shows
And I believe in the iron cross and as everybody knows
I believe in good time music, yeah, good time rock 'n' roll
I believe in music, music, music it'll satisfy your soul but
I believe in love (good-time music)

I believe in party time and I believe in soul
And I believe in temptation
And knock knock knockin' at your door
And I believe in good times, good times rock 'n' roll
Yeah I believe in the music, music, music
It'll satisfy your soul, don'tcha know that ah
I believe in love
Good time music
Good time rock 'n' roll

Banging on My Drum

I'm banging on my drum
I'm banging on my drum
I'm banging on my drum boy
Finding I'm having lots of fun
I'm banging on my drum yeah
I'm banging on my drum
I'm banging on my drum now babe
And I'm having lotsa fun

Follow the Leader

Follow, follow the leader, na-na-now
New York, New York City, na-na-na-na-na-now

Aw if you wanna dance
Hey work up a sweat and you baby better better get get yourself
a better little romance
Then you know you gotta get up a little sweat and get
a little romance
Then you'd better now follow, follow the leader na-na-now
New York, New York City na-na-na-na-na-now

You Wear It So Well

All of those things yeah that you've got to give
Yeah you wear it so well
Yeah you wear it so well
All of those stories honey that I know you could tell
Yeah you wear it so well
And your face hides it so I can't tell
That you knew it so well
You Wear It So Well
All of the things that made poets sing
You wear it so well, yeah, you hide it so well

And all of the pain that you used to tell
You hide it so well
Can't tell from your face that you knew it so well
Hey now that you had such a story to tell
Yeah you got style and grace and you wear it so well
You wear it so well and
You've got such a story to tell
You wear it so well
Grace and style
Equals you so well
You wear it so well

Ladies Pay

All the sailors they are all home for leave
And everybody's waiting for them to try to deceive
The storekeepers have drawn their lace curtains bare
And all the willowy young girls are waiting there
Ah but how the ladies pay
Oh if they only knew how the ladies pay
Here now, how the ladies pay
When the men they have gone away

Nobody is standing guard upon the door
And nobody is feeding any of the poor
The poor sick soldier lies in bed beside his girl
Thinking of another place on the other side of this world
Ah how the ladies pay
Oh how the ladies pay
When the men they have gone away
Oh I wish I knew how the ladies pay

Day and night
Night and day
How the ladies pay

Rock and Roll Heart

I don't like opera and I don't like ballet
And New Wave French movies they just drive me away
I guess I'm just dumb 'cause I knows I ain't smart
But deep down inside I've got a rock and roll heart
Yeah yeah yeah deep down inside I've got a rock and roll heart

A rock and roll heart
Searching for a good time
Just a rock and roll heart, roll heart, roll heart
Looking for a good time

I don't like messages or something meant to say
And I wish people like that would just go away
I guess that I'm dumb 'cause I know I'm not smart
But deep down inside I've got a rock and roll heart
Yeah, yeah, yeah deep down inside I've got a rock and roll heart

Senselessly Cruel

When I was a poor young boy in school
Girls like you always played me for a fool
But now the time has come to lay to waste
The theory people have of getting an acquired taste
You treated me oh so so senselessly cruel

From the beginning I suspected the worst
And you didn't disappoint me it's just that you were the first
But now I wouldn't let you touch me if you were within a foot
And girl I'm never ever gonna get hurt
'Cause you treated me oh so wrong
So senselessly cruel

Claim to Fame

Talk, talk, yak, yak
Watch out for that old one-track
Get it up and get it back
Makin' it upon your back

No space, no rent, the money's gone
It's all been spent now
Tell me 'bout your claim to fame
Now ain't that some claim to fame

Extra extra, read all about it now
Extra extra, something 'bout the claim to fame
Ooohhh sweet mama ooh sweet mama
Something 'bout a claim to fame

Wet lips, dry mouth
Ready for that old hand out now
Ain't that some claim to fame

Spaced out, spaced dead, the head is round
The square is pegged
Ain't that some claim to fame
Now tell me ain't that some claim to fame

Vicious Circle

You're caught in a vicious circle
Surrounded by your so-called friends
You're caught in a vicious circle
And it looks like it will never end
'Cause some people think that they like problems
And some people think that they don't
And for everybody who says yes
There's somebody whose starin' sayin' don't

You're caught in a vicious circle
Surrounded by your so-called friends
You're caught in a vicious circle
And it looks like it will just never end
'Cause some people think that it's nerves
And some people think that it's not
And some people think that it's things that you do
And others think that you were cold when you were hot
They think that that was what it was all about

You're caught in a vicious circle
Surrounded by all of your friends

A Sheltered Life

Never been to England
Never been to France
Never really learned how to dance
I've never taken dope
I've never taken drugs
I've never danced on a bear skin rug
Guess it's true what all those people they say
I'm gonna have to lose my hometown ways
Guess it's true
Guess I've led a sheltered life

Never went around with anything
I've had a home-town life and
I haven't ever learned to swing
Not much of a life
I haven't seen much
I've been true to my wife
And it's just been too much

Guess it's true
What all those people they say
I'm gonna have to lose my home-town ways
You know it's true
Guess I've led a sheltered life

Temporary Thing

Hey now bitch, now baby you'd better pack your things
Get outta here quick
Maybe your blood's gettin', ah, too rich
It ain't like we ain't never seen this thing before
And if it turns you, bend around
Then you'd better hit the door
But I know—it's just a temporary thing

You read too many books, you seen too many plays
And if things like this turn you away
Now look, hey look you'd better think about it twice
I know that your good breeding makes it seem not so nice
It's just a temporary thing

Where's the number, where's a dime and where's the phone
I feel like a stranger, I guess you're gonna go back home
Your mother, your father, your fucking brother
I guess they wouldn't agree with me
But I don't give two shits
They're no better than me

Uh huh,
It's just a temporary thing
Oh, yeah
Been there before, just a temporary thing
It's just a temporary thing
Ah bitch, get off my kids, temporary thing

Get out

It's just a temporary thing

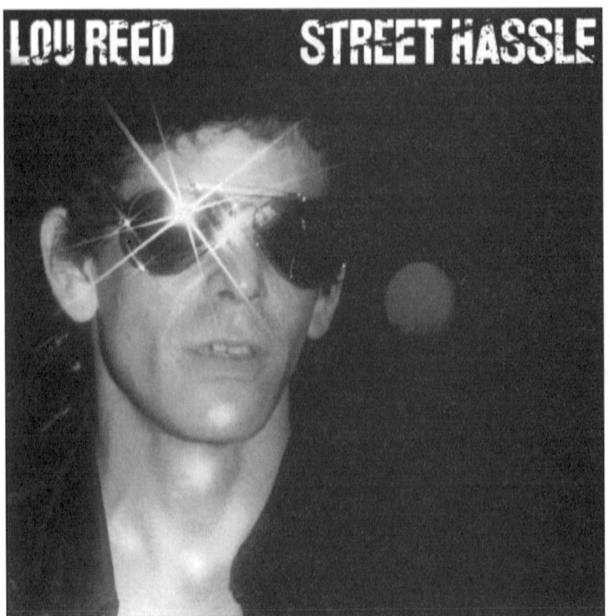
LOU REED
STREET HASSLE

Gimmie Some Good Times

“Hey, if it ain’t the Rock ’n’ Roll Animal himself.
What you doin’, bro?”
Standing on the corner
“Well I can see that. What you got in your hand?”
Suitcase in my hand
“No shit! What it is!”
Jack is in his corset, Jane is in her vest
“Fuckin’ ‘faggot’ ‘junkie’ ”
Sweet Jane, I’m in a rock and roll band
“Well, I can see that...”

Some people say that you can’t, no matter babe who you are
And some people say they can’t move, no matter where they are
Gimmie, gimmie, gimmie, some good times
Gimmie, Gimmie, Gimmie some pain
No matter how ugly you are, you know to me it all looks the same

Rain from the morning in the blue clouds
Now just shining up with dew
Riding through the city in the big cars
And me I ain’t got nothing to do
Gimmie, gimmie, gimmie some good times
Gimmie, gimmie, gimmie some pain
Don’t you know that things always look ugly
To me they always look the same
Don’t you know that both of them look ugly
To me they always look the same
Standing in the corner
To me they always look the same

Dirt (Final Version)

It's been a long time since I've spoken to you
Was it the right time?
Your current troubles and you know they'll get much worse
I hope you know how much I enjoyed them
You're a pig of a person, there's a justice in this world
Hey, how about that?
Your lack of conscience and your lack of morality
Well, more and more people know all about it

We sat around the other night, me and the guys,
Trying to find the right word
That would best fit and describe
You and people like you
That no principle has touched, no principles baptized
How about that?
Who'd eat shit and say it tasted good
If there was some money in it for 'em

Hey, you remember that song by this guy from Texas whose name was Bobby Fuller?
I'll sing it for you it went like this:
I fought the law and the law won
I fought the law and the law won

You're just dirt

Street Hassle: Waltzing Matilda, Part I

Waltzing Matilda whipped out her wallet
The sexy boy smiled in dismay
She took out four twenties 'cause she liked round figures
Everybody's queen for a day
Oh babe, I'm on fire and you know I admire your body
Why don't we slip away
Although I'm sure you're certain it's a rarity me flirtin'
Sha-la-la-la this way
Oh sha-la-la-la-la, sha-la-la-la-la
Hey baby, come on let's slip away

Luscious and gorgeous, oh what a muscle
Call out the National Guard
She creamed in her jeans as he picked up her means
From off of the formica topped bar
And cascading slowly, he lifted her wholly
And boldly out of this world
And despite people's derision
Proved to be more than a diversion sha-la-la-la later on—
And then sha-la-la-la-la he entered her slowly and showed her where he was coming from
And then sha-la-la-la-la he made love to her gently it was like she'd never ever come
And then sha-la-la-la-la sha-la-la-la-la
When the sun rose and he made to leave
You know sha-la-la-la-la sha-la-la-la-la
Neither one regretted a thing

Street Hassle: Street Hassle Part II

Hey that cunt's not breathing, I think she's had too much
Of something or other, hey man, you know what I mean?
I don't mean to scare you, but you're the one who came here
And you're the one who's got to take her when you leave
I'm not being smart or trying to be cold on my part
And I'm not gonna wear my heart on my sleeve
But you know, people get all emotional and sometimes, man
They just don't act rational they, you know,
They think they're on TV
Sha-la-la-la man, why don't you just slip away

You know, I'm glad that we met, man
It really was nice talking and I really wish that there was a little more time to speak
But you know, it could be a hassle trying to explain myself to a
Police officer about how it was your old lady got herself stiffed
And it's not like we could help her, there was nothing no one
Could do, and if there was man
You know I would have been the first
But when someone turns that blue, it is a universal truth
Then you just know that bitch will never fuck again
By the way, that's really some bad shit
That you came to our place with
But you ought to be more careful
Around the little girls

Lou Reed

Pass Thru Fire

It's either the best or it's the worst
And since I don't have to choose, I guess I won't
And I know this ain't no way to treat a guest
But why don't you grab your old lady by the feet
And just lay her out on the darkened street and by morning
She's just another hit-and-run

You know some people got no choice
And they can never find a voice
To talk with—
That they can even call their own
So the first thing that they see
That allows them the right to be
Why they follow it,
You know it's called—Bad Luck

Street Hassle: Slip Away, Part III

(Wait man, that's just a lie It's a lie she tells her friends there's a real song, a real song that she wouldn't even admit to herself, bleeding in her heart, it's a song lots of people moan, it's a painful song, with a lot of sad truths and life's full of sad songs, a penny for a wish, and wishing won't make it so Joe, where a pretty kiss, where a pretty face can't have its way, though tramps like us we were born to pay)

Love has gone away and there's no one here now and
There's nothing left to say but, oh how I miss him, baby
Ah baby, come on and slip away
Come on baby
Why don't you slip away
Love has gone away, took the rings off my fingers
And there's nothing left to say
But oh how, oh how I need it
Baby
Come on baby, I need you baby
Oh please don't slip away
I need your loving so bad
Babe
Please don't slip away

Lou Reed

Pass Thru Fire

I Wanna Be Black

I wanna be black
Have natural rhythm
Shoot twenty feet of jism, too
And fuck up the Jews
I wanna be black
I wanna be a Panther
Have a girlfriend named Samantha
And have a stable of foxy whores
Ooh I wanna be black
I don't wanna be a fucked-up, middle-class, college student anymore
I just want to have a stable of foxy little whores
Yeah, yeah I wanna be black

I wanna be black
I wanna be like Martin Luther King
And get myself shot in spring
Lead a whole generation too
And fuck up the Jews

I wanna be black, I wanna be like Malcolm X
And cast a hex over President Kennedy's tomb
And have a big prick, too

I don't wanna be a fucked-up, middle-class, college student no more

I just wanna have a stable of foxy little whores
Yeah, yeah I wanna be black

Real Good Time Together

We're gonna have a real good time together
We're gonna have a real good time together
We're gonna have a real good time together
We're gonna laugh and ball and shout together

Nah, nah, nah, nah, nah, nah, nah, nah, nah, nah, nah, nah, nah, nah

Shooting Star

All of the people had their share of the glory
Looking out after you
It's just a story about win, lose and glory
And you know that it's true
Uh-huh, oh yeah, you're just a shooting star
Uh-huh, oh yeah, you're just a shooting star

Some man-made glory won't permit the commission
Of another God
And later persuasion would permit rearranging
Of another bar
And to cause more confusion and to make a dis-illusion
Would have gone too far

And it's by admission a protracted admission
A cadillac metallic car
Uh huh, oh yeah, you're just a shooting star
Un huh, oh yeah, you're just a shooting star

Leave Me Alone

Everybody gonna try to tell you what to do, and
Never, never, never, never let it be said that it's true

Leave me, leave me, leave me, leave me
Leave me alone

Certain kinds of people they just always let you down
You're trying to go up and they just want a frown

Don't you know some people they just don't know when to stop
They can't tell the floor from the ceiling or the top
And then there's others types, they always make you wait
And they're the ones who always are the first to say, "Mistake"

Lonely lonely lonely lonely lonely boy
Leave me, leave me, leave me, leave me, leave me alone

Wait

(Disgrace
It was such a waste
Of such a pretty face)
Wait, I know I shouldn't, but please wait
I know the time is getting late
And he is lost who hesitates
But still I really wish that you would wait
Although this passion might abate
And find you in another state
That will see this as some mistake
Oh babe, I really think you ought to wait
Wait, I really wouldn't want your hate
Certainly not at this late date
You want to give not only take
I know propriety is such a weight
But then it makes no sense to wait
Considering the present state
Don't change my mind at this late date
Oh baby, don't you think we ought to wait

The Collected Lyrics

LOU REED THE BELLS

Stupid Man

Stupid man, hitchhiking out of a good life in Saskatchewan
And he thinks he's got big, big plans
Gonna build a house upon some land
Oh Casey, don't it make you crazy
Oh when you're livin' all alone by that damn water
Oh Casey, don't it make you crazy
When you're livin' all alone by those still waters
Please say hello, please say hello, to my little baby daughter
Oh Casey tell her that her father's gonna be coming home so soon,
so soon, to see her
Well I'm shooting down the turnpike
With the driver doin' 95 or maybe more
Don't you think he's loaded, drunk
Or that he thinks that life's a bore
Oh Casey, oh Casey, don't you know how it makes me so damn crazy
Livin' all alone by those waters
But please say hello, but please say hello to my little baby daughter
Please please won't you just give her a great big kiss then tell her
That her stupid daddy will be coming home soon
Oh Casey, oh Casey, don't you know I made me so damn crazy
When I was livin' there all alone by those still waters
But please tell my baby baby baby baby daughter
That I'm tied up now but I'll be home soon
And I'll be the daddy that I oughta
Please say hello, from a stupid man

Disco Mystic

Disco, disco mystic

I Wanna Boogie With You

Hey pretty baby, don't you think you might give me a chance
Get it on with me, go downtown for some love and romance
And I know I ain't nothing, I ain't worth but a thin dime
But if you put your heart in my hands
I'm sure that I could change your mind

I wanna boogie with you, yeah, I wanna boogie with you

And there is something, baby that your parents both agreed
(They did agree)
And that is that they both had it, a big distrust in me
(Distrusted me)
And your best friend Frankie, I know your best friend Frankie
Wants to see me sink (wants to see me sink) and I don't much
   blame him for that
He gets so useless after so few drinks

You know babe, I wanna boogie with you

And I know your little baby sister she thinks that I'm a flop
   (thinks that I'm a flop)
But I guess that you know that it's true
I spent more time on the bottom than the top
   (bottom than the top)
Tell your little sister I know she wants to give me a whirl
   (give me a whirl)
But I don't have the time, babe wait till she's grown up and she's
   a woman, not a girl
Don't you know I want to boogie with you
Down on the corner

With You

With you, life moves so fast
With you, everything's a mess
Slow down
Don't you think you could be less capricious
I'm not you, I don't have no death wish
Slow down, slow down
With you, there is no denying
It's you, not my lack of trying
With you everybody's lying
It's you, it's not me who's crying

With you, stay and hold tightly from the streets
With you, every friend's a possible beat
Slow down, slow down
With you, it's a foregone conclusion
With you, envy, it's all a delusion
With you, I can have no illusion
It's you, who has the contusions
Crying

With you, everyone's a sucker
With you, it's fuckee or fucker
Slow down, slow down

With you, life is just a scramble
With you, every day is a gamble
With you, I can forget life barely
With you, playing the Virgin Mary
And you're crying

Looking for Love

Hey now, there's a lovely girl and she's stealin' all your sheets
Hey now, there's a lovely girl that's the kind of girl to meet
Hey now, there's a lonely boy and he's looking looking for love
Now, there's a lovely girl and she's looking for a stud
Hey now, won't you give it now
Won't you give it give it give it to me
Hey now there's a lucky girl give it give it give it to me

Hey now, there's an international boy walking around the world
Hey now, there's a jet-set star looking still for some little pick-up girl
I said hey now, you used to scratch my back
And you look across the board
Hey now, when you ripped open my shirt
You see that's written hey "The Wanderer" on my chest
Hey now, there's a lovely girl
Easy kiss kisses goodbye
Hey now, there's a lovely child look look looking for love

City Lights

Don't these city lights light these streets to life
Don't these crazy nights bring us together
Any rainy day, you can dance those blues away
Don't these city lights bring us together

Charlie Chaplin's cane, well it flicked away the rain
Things weren't quite the same, after he came here
But then when he left, upon our own request
Things weren't quite the same, after he came here

We're supposed to be
A land of liberty
And those city lights to blaze forever
But that little tramp, leaning on that street corner lamp
When he left us, his humor left us forever

Don't these city lights bring these streets to life
Don't these crazy nights bring us together
Any rainy day, you can dance those blues away
Don't these city lights bring us together

All Through The Night

Don't you feel so lonely when it's in the afternoon
And you gotta face it all through the night
Don't it make you believe that something's gonna have to
 happen soon, oh baby
All through the night

Have you ever played with an all-night band
And gone through it, baby all through the night
When the daytime descends in a nighttime of hell
 everybody's gone to look for a bell to ring
All through the night
And they do it all through the night

When the words were down and the poetry comes and
 the novel's written and the book is done you said oh lord,
 lover baby give it to me all through the night and she says it

My best friend Sally, she got sick
And I'm feeling mighty ill myself
It happens all the time and all through the night
I went to St. Vincent's and I'm watching the ceiling
 fall down on the body as she's lying there on
the ground
Says oh baby, gotta celebrate all through the night
Made me feel so sad I cried all through the night
I said oh Jesus, all through the night

If the sinners sin and the good man's gone and a woman can't come
And help him home and what you gonna do about it
When they go on all through the night
And he says give it to me all through the night

It ain't so much when a man's gotta cry, give a little loving
And some piece of mind
I said hey babe, give it to me all through the night

And some people wait for things that never come
And some people dream of things that never been done
They do it all through the night
The city's funny and the country's quiet but I'd wanna know
  why they don't have a riot
Why don't they do it, baby
All through the night

Oh mama, oh mama tell me about it all through the night
I want to have it all through the night
If Christmas comes only once a year
Why can't anybody shed just one tear
For things that don't happen all through the night

Families

Mama, you tell me how's the family
And mama, tell me how's things going by you
And little baby sister, I heard that you got married
And I heard that you had yourself a little baby girl, too
And here's some uncles and some cousins I know vaguely
And would you believe my old dog Chelsy's there, too
And would you believe nobody in this family wanted to keep her
And now that dog's more a part of this family than I am too
I don't come home much anymore
No I don't come home much anymore

And mama, I know how disappointed you are
And papa, I know that you feel the same way too
And no, I still haven't got married
And no, there's no grandson
Planned here for you
And by the way daddy, tell me how's the business
I understand that your stock she's growing very high
No daddy, you're not a poor man anymore
And I hope you realize that
Before you die

Please, come on let's not start this business again
I know how much you resent the life that I have

But one more time I don't want the family business
Don't want to inherit it upon the day that you die
Really dad, you should have given it to my sister
You know, Elizabeth, you know Elizabeth
She has a better head for those things than I
She lives practically around the corner
That's really the kind of child you could be proud of

But papa, I know that this visit's a mistake
There's nothing here we have in common except our name
And families that live out in the suburbs
Often make each other cry

And I don't think that I'll come home much anymore
No, no I don't think I'll come home much again

Mama, Papa

The Bells

And the actresses relate
To the actor who comes home late
After the plays have gone down
And the crowds have scattered around
Through the city lights and the streets
No ticket could be beat
For the beautiful show of shows
Ah, Broadway only knows
The Great White Milky Way
It had something to say
When he fell down on his knees
After soaring through the air
With nothing to hold him there
It was really not so cute
To play without a parachute
As he stood upon the ledge
Looking out he thought he saw a brook—

And he hollered, "Look! There are the bells!"
And he sang out, "Here come the bells!"
"Here come the bells!"
"Here come the bells!"

Here comes the bells

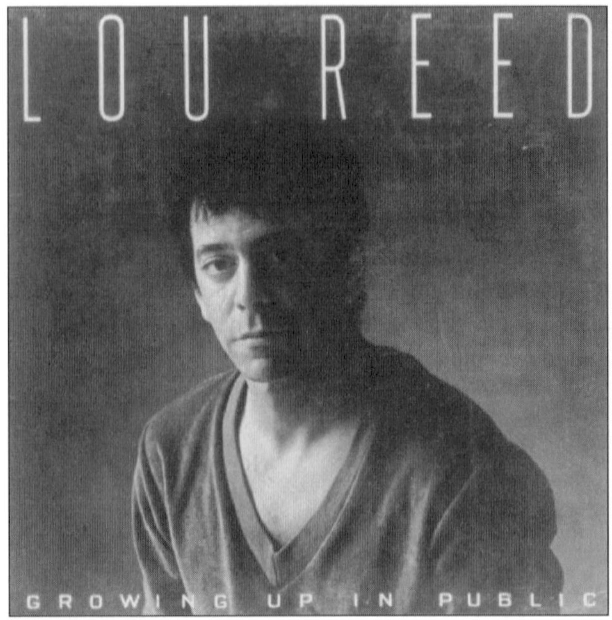
LOU REED
GROWING UP IN PUBLIC

How Do You Speak to An Angel

A son who is cursed with a harridan mother
Or a weak simpering father at best
Is raised to play out the timeless classical motives
Of filial love and incest

How does he
Speak to a
How does he speak to the prettiest girl
How does he
Talk to her
What does he say for an opening line
What does he say if he's shy

What do you do with your pragmatic passions
With your classically neurotic style
How do you deal with your vague self-comprehension
What do you do when you lie

How do you
Speak to a
How do you speak to the prettiest girl
How do you speak to her
How do you dance on the head of a pin
When you're on the outside looking in

My Old Man

When I was a young boy in Brooklyn going to public school
During recess in the concrete playground they lined us up by twos
In alphabetical order, Reagan, Reed, and Russo
I still remember the names
And stickball and stoopball
Were the only games that we played
And I wanted to be like my old man
I wanted to grow up to be like my old man
I wanted to dress like, I wanted to be just like
I wanted to act like my old man

And then like everyone else I started to grow
And I didn't want to be like my father anymore
I was sick of his bullying
And having to hide under a desk on the floor
And when he beat my mother, it made me so mad I could choke
And I didn't want to be like my old man
I didn't even want to look like my old man
I didn't even want to seem like my old man

A son watches his father, being cruel to his mother
And makes a vow to return only when
He is so much richer, in every way so much bigger
That the old man will never hit anyone again.

And can you believe what he said to me
He said, Lou, act like a man

Keep Away

You keep your jealousy and your snide remarks to yourself
You know that I'm not seeing anybody else
You just keep your ear down to the ground
Yell your head off if you hear a sound
And here's a whistle, and a badge and a phone
You can arrest me if I'm not at home
And if I don't keep my word I swear I'll keep away

Here's some books and a puzzle by Escher
Here's Shakespeare's "Measure for Measure"
Here's a balloon, a rubber band and a bag
Why don't you blow them up, if you think you've been had
Here's a castle, a paper dragon and a moat
An earring, a toothbrush and a cloak
And if I don't keep my word I swear I'll keep away

I swear I'll keep away
From all we've ever done
I'll keep away the good times and
I'll keep away the fun
I swear I'll join the army or maybe the marines
I'll start to wear designer suits and put away my jeans
I swear that I'll keep away from all my old time friends
I'll throw away my records I'll try to make amends
I swear I'll give up gambling and playing with the rent
I'll give up food and drinking I'll give up a life ill spent

Here's a yardstick you can measure me by
Here's a coupon, maybe there's something you want to buy
Here's a Band-Aid in case you cut your feet
Here's a rubber mallet you can use on your front teeth
Here's a gun no one uses anymore
And a bracelet made of some inexpensive ore
And if I don't keep my word you won't see me anymore

I swear I'll keep away from dignity and pride
I'll keep away from abstracts I'll keep it all inside
Well, I'll just wrap me up in butter and melt me on a shelf
I'll fry in my own juices I'll become somebody else

Well, I'll just swear to keep away from everything that's good
I'll lie down in the gutter where I really should
I swear I'll light a candle to every modern foe
I swear I'll close the book on this and not see you anymore
    'cause I just gotta get away

Growing Up In Public

Some people are into the power of power
The absolute corrupting power, that makes great men insane
While some people find their refreshment in action
The manipulation, encroachment and destruction of their inferiors

Growing Up in Public   Growing Up in Public
Growing Up in Public   Growing Up in Public
With your pants down

Some people are into their sadistic pleasures
They whet your desires and they drool in your ears
They're quasieffeminate characters in love with oral gratification
They edify your integrity, so they can play on your fears

And they're gonna do it in public   'Cause you're Growing Up in Public
They're gonna do it to you in public   'Cause you're Growing Up in Public
With your pants down

Some people think being a man is unmanly
And then some people think that whole concept's a joke
But some people think being a man is the whole point
And then some people wish that they'd never awoke
Up from a dream of nightmarish proportions
Down to a size neither regal nor calm
A Prince Hamlet caught in the middle between reason and instinct
Caught in the middle with your pants down again

Caught in the middle
I'm really caught in the middle
I'm caught in the middle
Caught in the middle baby deciding about you

Standing On Ceremony

Remember your manners
Will you please take your hat off
Your mother is dying
Listen to her cough

We were always standing on ceremony
We were always standing on ceremony

Can't you show some respect please
Although you didn't in real life
Your mother is dying
And I god damn well hope you're satisfied

We were always standing on ceremony
We were always standing on ceremony

So please play another song on that juke box
Please play another pretty sad song for me
And if that phone rings
Tell them that you haven't seen me
If'n that phone rings
Tell them you haven't seen me for weeks
And this one here's on me
Standing on ceremony

So Alone

She calls on the phone
She says she doesn't want to be alone
She says it's making her neurotic
But please don't mistake it for being erotic
So alone
So all alone

She says let's go for a walk
We'll have a drink and maybe we will talk
And he thinks she has possibilities
If she could just put away her rosary
So all alone
Nobody wants to be alone

But I just didn't know
I swear to you, I just didn't know
I would never make you sad
If I had known
I never would have said those things to you
You'd have to be crazy to say those things to you

Let's face it, I made a mistake
Well you know, fools rush in where angels take a break
I can't be smart all of the time
And anyway I didn't know you were marking time over him
To tell you the truth
I forgot all about him

And you know I don't think it's nice
Asking one man about another man's vice
I don't care if you pick my head
As long as we end up in bed—alone
Just the two of us alone

I just didn't know
I swear to God, I just didn't know
Can't you understand that it's frightening
When you hear women talking about castrating and hating men
Who wants to know about how you hate men

Well you said now you wanted to dance
So now we're going to dance
You said that you weren't complete
But we're going to put you on your feet
You said that you were very vexed
And you told me to forget about sex
You said you liked me for my mind
Well, I really love your behind

Oh get up and boogie, oh baby get up and dance
Oh get get get get up and boogie baby, oh get up and dance
Shake your booty mama, oh get up and dance

Your point's very clear
You're not one to cry into your beer
Why don't we go to my place
Believe me, I'm very chaste
And I'm so alone
So all alone

Sure, all men are beasts
Hey look, I'll sit here quietly and I'll stare at my feet
I don't blame you for taking umbrage
With animals staring at your cleavage
So alone
We're so all alone

Hey, do you mind if I turn out the light
Don't take offense, but why don't you spend the night
I know your passions run very deep
But at this point we both need sleep
So alone
And who wants to be alone

Love Is Here To Stay

They both love Chinese food, he hates to dress
He loves to play pinball, she wants to play next
She likes her novels long, he's into comic books
They're gilt-edged polymorphous urban but
somehow it works

She likes Truman Capote, he likes Gore Vidal
He likes Edgar Allan Poe, and she's into Mean Joe Greene
She thinks eating meat's disgusting, he likes hot dogs
She's into Gestalt therapy, while Est and the rest
just make him ill, but

Love is here, here to stay
Love is here, here to stay
It gets proven every day
Love is here, here to stay

The Power Of Positive Drinking

Some like wine and some like hops
But what I really love is my scotch
It's the power, the power of positive drinking
Some people ruin their drinks with ice
And then, they, they ask you for advice
They tell you, I've never told this to anyone before.
They say, Candy is dandy but liquor makes quipsters
And I don't like mixers, or sippers or sob sisters
You know, you have to be real careful
Where you sit down in a bar these days
And then some people drink to unleash their libidos
And other people drink to prop up their egos
It's my burden, man
People say I have the kind of face you can trust

Some people say alcohol makes you less lucid
And I think that's true if you're kind of stupid
I'm not that kind that gets himself burned twice
And some say liquor kills the cells in your head
And for that matter so does getting out of bed
When I exit, I'll go out gracefully, shot in my hand

Smiles

Smiles—I was taught never to smile
I was told the stylish smiles of buffoonery and chicanery and larceny abound
My mom said unless someone sticks you right in front of a camera
A smile is the last thing that you wanna do
Those smiles—those mirthless toothy smiles

Smiles—they all smile on TV
The quizmaster with his withered crones
The talk show hosting movie stars
The politician licking feet
The mugger, the rapist,
The arsonist lover
All smile out from the news
At one time or another
Those smiles—those garish, sickly smiles

When I was young my mother said to me—
"Never, ever, let anyone see that you're happy"
Smiles, never, ever let them see you smile—
They'll always put you down—with those smiles—
Never, ever let them see you smile—
They'll always put you down—with your smiles—
Never, ever, let them see you smile—
They'll always put you down—with your smiles—
Never, ever let them see you smile—
Don't you know they'll make you go:
Doo doo doo doo doo doo doo doo
Doo doo doo doo doo doo doo doo
Doo

Think It Over

Waking, he stared raptly at her face
On his lips, her smell, her taste
Black hair framing her perfect face
With her wonderful mind and her incredible grace
And so, he woke he woke her with a start
To offer her his heart
Once and for all, forever to keep
And the words that she first heard him speak
Were really very sweet
He was asking her to marry him, and to think it over
Baby think it over

She said somewhere there's a faraway place
Where all is ordered and all is grace
No one there is ever disgraced
And everybody there is wise and everyone has taste
And then she sighed, well la-dee-dah-dee-dah
You and I have come quite far
And we really must watch what we say
Because when you ask for someone's heart
You must know that you're smart
Smart enough to care for it
So I'm gonna think it over
Baby, I'm going to think it over

Teach The Gifted Children

Teach the gifted children, teach them to have mercy
Teach them about sunsets, teach them about moonrise
Teach them about anger, the sin that comes with dawning
Teach them about flowers and the beauty of forgetfulness
Then take me to the river and put me in the water
Bless them and forgive them, Father cause they just don't know

All the gifted children, teach the gifted children
The ways of men and animals
Teach them about cities, the history of the mysteries
Their vices and their virtues
About branches that blow in the wind
Or the wages of their sins
Teach them of forgiveness, teach them about mercy
Teach them about music
And the cool and cleansing water
Teach the gifted children
All the gifted children

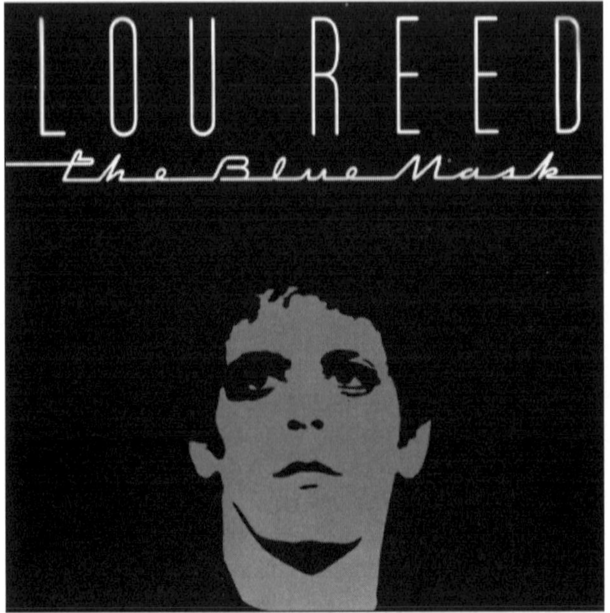
LOU REED
The Blue Mask

My House

The image of the poet's in the breeze
Canadian geese are flying above the trees
A mist is hanging gently on the lake
My house is very beautiful at night
My friend and teacher occupies a spare room
He's dead—at peace at last the wandering Jew
Other friends had put stones on his grave
He was the first great man that I had ever met
Sylvia and I got out our Ouija Board
To dial a spirit—across the room it soared
We were happy and amazed at what we saw
Blazing stood the proud and regal name Delmore
Delmore, I missed all your funny ways
I missed your jokes and the brilliant things you said
My Daedalus to your Bloom, was such a perfect wit
And to find you in my house makes things perfect
I've really got a lucky life
My writing, my motorcycle, and my wife
And to top it all off a spirit of pure poetry
Is living in this stone and wood house with me
The image of the poet's in the breeze
Canadian geese are flying above the trees
A mist is hanging gently on the lake
Our house is very beautiful at night

Women

I love women
I think they're great
They're a solace to a world in a terrible state
They're a blessing to the eyes
A balm to the soul
What a nightmare to have no women in the world

I used to look at women in the magazines
I know that it was sexist but I was in my teens
I was very bitter, all my sex was on the sly
I couldn't keep my hands off women
And I won't till I die

A woman's love can lift you up and women can inspire
I feel like buying flowers and hiring a celestial choir
A choir of castratis to serenade my love
They'd sing a little Bach for us and then we'd make love

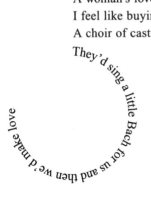

I love women
We all love women
We love women

Underneath the Bottle

Oooh wheee, look at me
Looking for some sympathy
It's the same old story—of man and his search for glory
And he found it, there underneath the bottle
Things are never good
Things go from bad to weird
Hey gimmie another scotch with my beer
I'm sad to say I feel the same today—as I always do
Gimmie a drink to relax me
Oooh wheee, liquor set me free
I can't do no work, with these shakes inside me
Awww fuck, I got the lousiest luck
I'm sick of this, underneath the bottle
Seven days make a week, on two of them I sleep
I can't remember what the hell I was doin'
I got bruises on my leg from I can't remember when
I fell down some stairs I was lyin' underneath the bottle
Ooooh wheee
Son of a B
You get so down you can't get any lower
So long world you play too rough
And it's getting me all mixed up
I lost my pride and it's hidin'
There—
Underneath the bottle

The Gun

The man has a gun
He knows how to use it
Nine millimeter Browning, let's see what he can do
He'll point it at your mouth
Says that he'll blow your brains out
Don't you mess with me
I'm carrying a gun
Carrying a gun
Carrying a gun
Don't you mess with me
Carrying a gun
Get over there
Move slowly
I'll put a hole in your face
If you even breathe a word
Tell the lady to lie down
I want you to be sure to see this
I wouldn't want you to miss a second
Watch your wife
Carrying a gun
Shooting with a gun
Dirty animal

Carrying a gun
Carrying a gun
Watch your face
Carrying a gun
Carrying a gun
Carrying a gun

The animal dies with fear in his eyes
With a gun
Don't touch him
Don't touch him
Stay away from him
He's got a gun

The Blue Mask

They tied his arms behind his back to teach him how to swim
They put blood in his coffee and milk in his gin
They stood over the soldier in the midst of the squalor
There was war in his body and it caused his brain to holler

M a k e t h e s a c r i f i c e
M u t i l a t e m y f a c e
If you need someone to kill
I'm a man without a will
W a s h t h e r a z o r i n t h
Let me luxuriate in pain
Please don't set me free
D e a t h m e a n s a l o t t o m e

The pain was lean and it made him scream
He knew he was alive
They put a pin through the nipples on his chest
He thought he was a saint
I've made love to my mother, killed my father and my brother
W h a t I a m t o d o
When a sin goes too far, it's like a runaway car
It cannot be controlled
Spit upon his face and scream
There's no Oedipus today
This is no play you're thinking you are in
W h a t w i l l y o u s a y

Take the blue mask down from my face and look me in the eye
I get a thrill from punishment
I've always been that way
I loathe and despise repentance
You are permanently stained
Your weakness buys indifference
And indescretion in the streets
Dirty's what you are and clean is what you're not
You deserve to be soundly beat

ain

Make the sacrifice
Take it all the way
There's no "won't" high enough
To stop this desperate day
Don't take death away
Cut the finger at the joint
Cut the stallion at his mount
And stuff it in his mouth

I ain't no Christian or no born-again saint
I ain't no cowboy or a Marxist D.A.
I ain't no criminal or Reverend Cripple from the right
I am just your average guy, trying to do what's right
I'm just your average guy

An average guy—I'm just your average guy
I'm average looking and I'm average inside
I'm an average lover and I live in an average place
You wouldn't know me if you met me face to face
I'm just your average guy
I'm just an average guy

I worry about money and taxes and such
I worry that my liver's big and it hurts to the touch
I worry about my health and bowels
And the crime waves in the street
I'm really just your average guy
Trying to stand on his own two feet
I'm just your average guy

Average looks
Average tastes
Average height
An average waist
Average in everything I do
My temperature is 98.2
I'm just your average guy

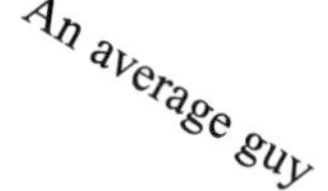

The Heroine

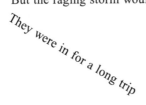

The heroine stood up on the deck
The ship was out of control
The bow was being ripped to shreds
Men were fighting down below
The sea had pummeled them for so long
That they knew nothing but fear
And the baby's in his box, he thinks the door is locked
The sea is in a state, the baby learns to wait
For the heroine
Locked in his defense
He waits for the heroine

The mast is cracking as the waves are slapping
Sailors rolled across the deck
And when they thought no one was looking
They would cut a weaker man's neck
While the heroine dressed
In a virgin white dress
Tried to steer the mighty ship
But the raging storm wouldn't hear of it

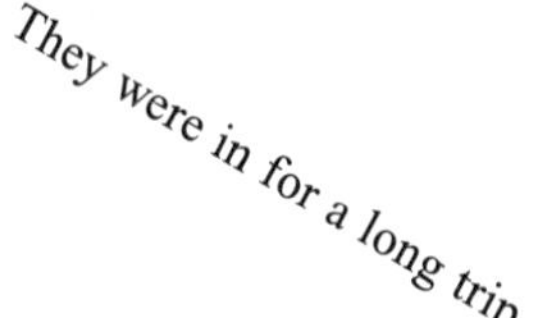
They were in for a long trip

Baby's in a box, thinks the door is locked
He finds it hard to breathe, drawing in the sea
And where's the heroine
To fire off the gun
To calm the raging seas
And let herself be seized by
The baby in the box
He thinks the door is locked
The woman has the keys
But there's no moment she can seize

Here's to the heroine
Who transcends all the men
Who are locked inside the box
Will the lady let him out—

The Heroine
Strapped to the mast
The pale ascendant
H e r o i n e

Waves of Fear

Waves of fear attack in the night
Waves of revulsion—sickening sights
My heart's nearly bursting
My chest's choking tight
Waves of fear, waves of fear

Waves of fear
Squat on the floor
Looking for some pill, the liquor is gone
Blood drips from my nose, I can barely breathe
Waves of fear I'm too scared to leave

I'm too afraid to use the phone
I'm too afraid to put the light on
I'm so afraid I've lost control
I'm suffocating without a word
Crazy with sweat, spittle on my jaw
What's that funny noise,
What's that on the floor
Waves of fear
Pulsing with death
I curse at my tremors
I jump at my own step
I cringe at my terror
I hate my own smell
I know where I must be
I must be in hell

Waves of fear
Waves of fear

The Day John Kennedy Died

I dreamed I was the president of these United States
I dreamed I replaced ignorance, stupidity and hate
I dreamed the perfect union and the perfect law, undenied
And most of all I dreamed I forgot the day John Kennedy died

I dreamed that I could do the job that others hadn't done
I dreamed that I was uncorrupt and fair to everyone
I dreamed I wasn't gross or base, a criminal on the take
And most of all I dreamed I forgot the day John Kennedy died

I remember where I was that day I was upstate in a bar
The team from the university was playing football on TV
Then the screen went dead and the announcer said
"There's been a tragedy, there are unconfirmed reports the
President's been shot, and he may be dead or dying."
Talking stopped, someone shouted, "What?!"
I ran out to the street
People were gathered everywhere saying did you hear
    what they said on TV
And then a guy in a Porsche with his radio on
Hit his horn and told us the news
He said, "The president's dead, he was shot twice in the head
In Dallas, and they don't know by whom."

I dreamed I was the president of these United States
I dreamed that I was young and smart and it was not a waste
I dreamed that there was a point to life and to the human race
I dreamed that I could somehow comprehend that someone
Shot him in the face

Oh, the day John Kennedy died

Heavenly Arms

Heavenly arms reach out to hold me
Heavenly arms entice you to dance
In a world of ill will, the dancers are still
Heavenly arms reach out to me

Heavenly arms soft as a love song
Heavenly arms bring a kiss to your ear
In a world that seems mad
All the dancers seem sad
Heavenly arms reach out to me

Heavenly arms come to my rescue
Only a woman can love a man
In a world full of hate love should never wait
Heavenly arms reach out to me

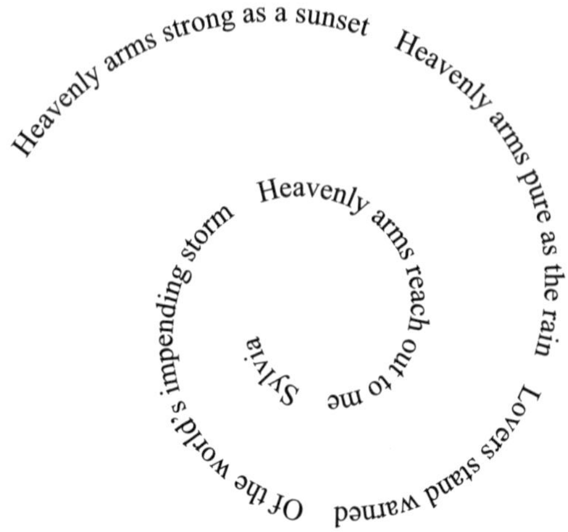

Heavenly arms strong as a sunset
Heavenly arms pure as the rain
Lovers stand warned
Of the world's impending storm
Heavenly arms reach out to me
Sylvia

LOU
REED
Legendary
Hearts

Legendary Hearts

Legendary hearts, tearing us apart
With stories of their love
The great transcendent loves
While we stand here and fight
And lose another night of legendary love

Legendary loves, haunt me in my sleep
Promises to keep, I never should have made
I can't live up to this
I'm good for just a kiss—not legendary love

Romeo oh Romeo, wherefore art thou Romeo
He's in a car or at a bar
Or churning his blood with an impure drug
He's in the past and seemingly lost forever
He worked hard at being good
But his basic soul was stained not pure
And when he took his bow no audience was clapping

Legendary hearts, tear us all apart
Make our emotions bleed, crying out in need
No legendary love is coming from above
It's in this room right now

And you've got to fight to make what's right
You've got to fight to keep your legendary love

Don't Talk to Me About Work

A perfect day to get out of bed
Shower, dress, shave, kiss you on the head
Then I hit the office and my head starts to swim
A perfect day to just walk around
See a violent movie check the sounds
But even on the street when I hear a phone ring
My heart starts to beat
When I get home I don't want you to speak

Don't talk to me about work
Please, don't talk to me about work
I'm up to my eyeballs in dirt—
With work, with work

How many dollars
How many sales
How many liars
How many tales
How many insults must you take in this one life

I'm in prison most of the day
So please excuse me if I get this way
But I have got obligations to keep
So be very careful when you speak
Don't talk to me about work
Please don't talk to me about work
I'm up to my eyeballs in dirt—
With work, with work
Please, don't talk to me about work
Don't you talk to me about work
I'm up to my eyeballs in dirt
With work, with work

MAKE up my MIND

~~Make Up My Mind~~

I CAN'T to SEEM TO MAKE UP my MIND

~~I can't seem to make up my mind~~ I CAN'T TELL the COLORS
~~I can't tell the colors that will fit this room~~ THAT WILL FIT THIS ROOM
~~I can't tell a thing about you~~ I CAN'T tell A THING ABOUT YOU
~~Make up my mind~~ MAKE UP MY MIND

~~I can't seem to make up my mind~~ I CAN'T SEEM TO MAKE UP MY MIND
~~Are you laughing at me or telling a joke~~? ARE YOU LAUGHING AT ME OR TELLING A JOKE?
~~The cigarette on the sheet begins to smoke~~ THE CIGARETTE on the SHEET BEGINS TO SMOKE
~~Make up your mind~~ MAKE UP YOUR MIND

Right or left, up or down, in or out, straight or round
Love or lust, rain or shine
I can't seem to make up my poor mind

I can't seem to make up my mind
I can't tell the difference between wrong and right
Are you laughing at me in your sleep tonight?
Leaving me behind—
WHY DON'T YOU MAKE UP YOUR MIND
~~Why don't you make up your mind~~
~~About leaving me behind~~

ABOUT LEAVING ME BEHIND

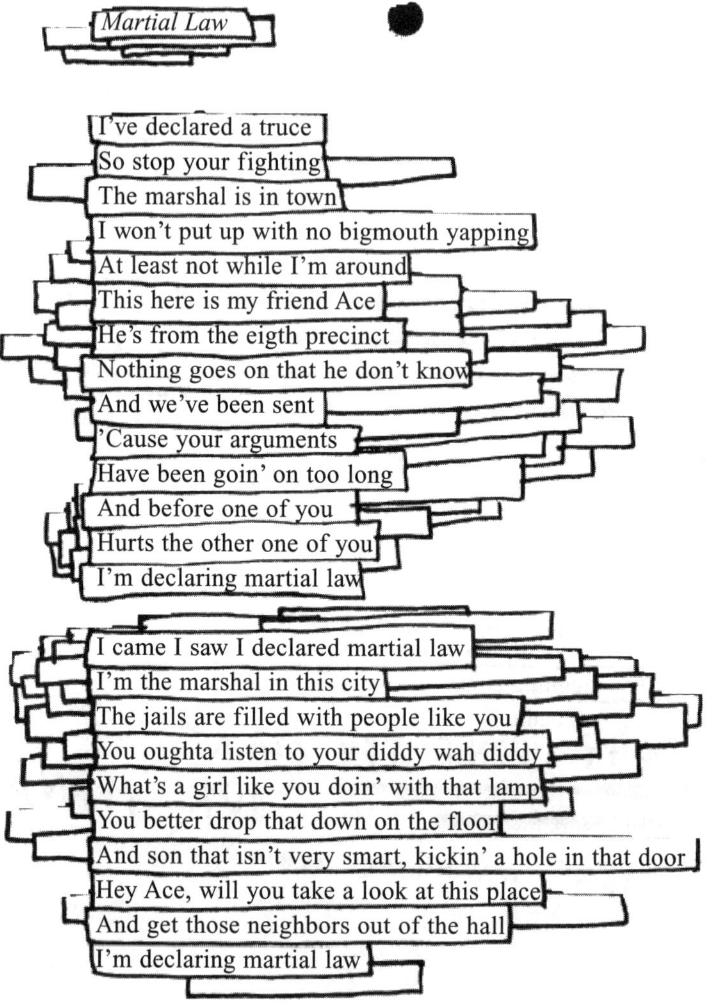

Martial Law

I've declared a truce
So stop your fighting
The marshal is in town
I won't put up with no bigmouth yapping
At least not while I'm around
This here is my friend Ace
He's from the eigth precinct
Nothing goes on that he don't know
And we've been sent
'Cause your arguments
Have been goin' on too long
And before one of you
Hurts the other one of you
I'm declaring martial law

I came I saw I declared martial law
I'm the marshal in this city
The jails are filled with people like you
You oughta listen to your diddy wah diddy
What's a girl like you doin' with that lamp
You better drop that down on the floor
And son that isn't very smart, kickin' a hole in that door
Hey Ace, will you take a look at this place
And get those neighbors out of the hall
I'm declaring martial law

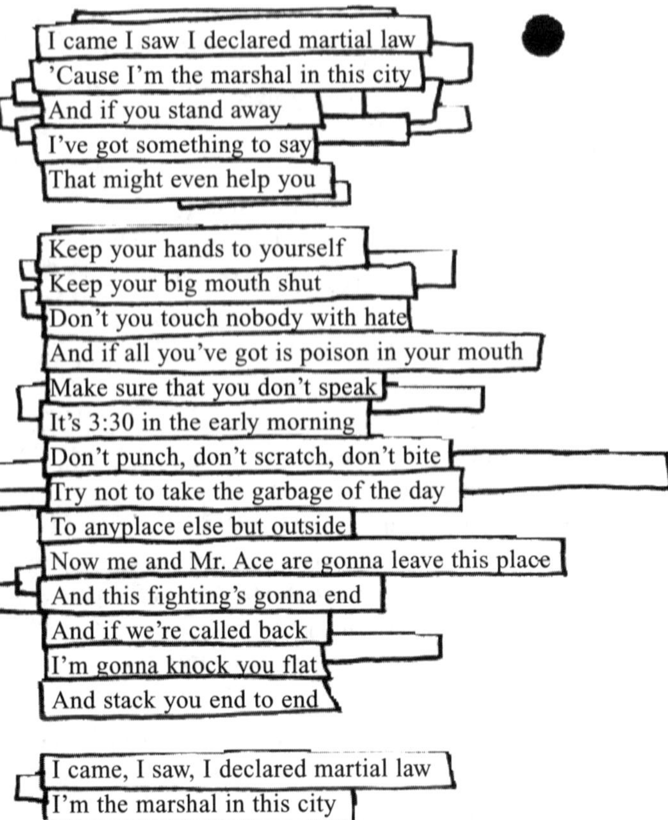

I came I saw I declared martial law
'Cause I'm the marshal in this city
And if you stand away
I've got something to say
That might even help you

Keep your hands to yourself
Keep your big mouth shut
Don't you touch nobody with hate
And if all you've got is poison in your mouth
Make sure that you don't speak
It's 3:30 in the early morning
Don't punch, don't scratch, don't bite
Try not to take the garbage of the day
To anyplace else but outside
Now me and Mr. Ace are gonna leave this place
And this fighting's gonna end
And if we're called back
I'm gonna knock you flat
And stack you end to end

I came, I saw, I declared martial law
I'm the marshal in this city

The Last Shot

The last shot should have killed me,
Pour another drink
Let's drink to the last shot
And the blood on the dishes in the sink
Blood inside the coffee cup, blood on the table top
But when you quit, you quit
But you always wish
That you knew it was your last shot
I shot blood at the fly on the wall
My heart almost stopped, hardly there at all
I broke the mirror with my fall, with my fall-fall-fall
Gimmie a double, give yourself one, too
Gimmie a short beer, and one for you, too
And a toast to everything that doesn't move, that doesn't move
But when you quit, you quit
But you always wish that you knew it was your last shot
But when you quit, you quit
But you always wish that you knew it was your last shot
Whisky, bourbon, vodka, scotch
I don't care what it is you've got
I just want to know that it's my last shot, my last shot
I remember when I quit pretty good

See this here's where I chipped my tooth
I shot a vein in my neck and I coughed up a Quaalude on
My last shot,
Here's a toast to all that's good and here's a toast to hate
And here's a toast to toasting and I'm not boasting
When I say I'm getting straight, when I say I'm getting straight

But when you quit, you quit
But you always wish, that you knew it was
Your last shot
When you quit, you quit
But you always wish
That you knew it was your last shot

TURN OUT the LIGHT

Lover, lover why is there light
In the itchy-gitchy evening and it's dark outside
And what is the difference between wrong and right
Wrong and right
Isn't it funny how pain goes away
And then comes back another day
The air feels very good today
Good today

Lover, lover why is there light
Did you forget to turn off that light
Well that's all right but it was way too bright
Way too bright
See the eagle above the hill
The lake reflects and is so still
The tension has gone from my will
From my will

Moon on the mountain shining bright
First there's dark and then there's light
And sometimes the light is way too bright
It's way too bright

Why don't you turn off the light?
Turn off the light

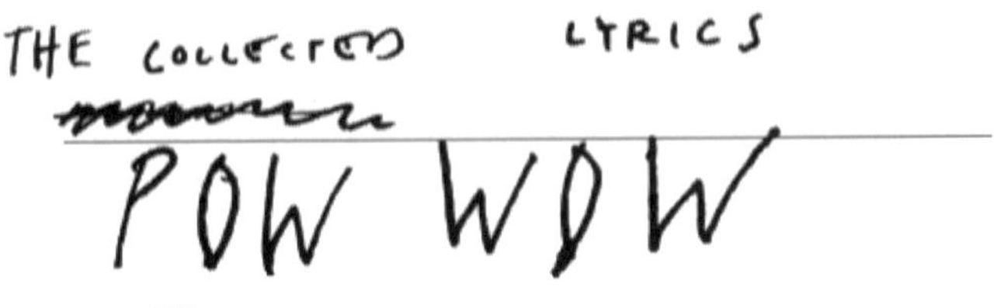

Christopher Columbus discovered America
Found he had a cornucopia
Gave love to the Indians and they gave it back
A pow wow in the teepee is where it's at

I want to dance with you
I want to dance with you
I want to dance with you
I want to dance with you
The Indian fought with his arrow and his bow
Till General Custer lost to Sitting Bull
Scalped all day and scalped all night
Give me that fire water
I'm gonna buy me a wife

I want to dance with you
I want to dance with you
I want to dance with you
I want to dance with you
When your people first moved to our block
Our ancestors met with culture shock
Two different monkeys from two different trees
Come on let's stop our fightin'
And come dance with me

Come on and dance with me
Come on and dance with me
'Cause I really want to dance with you
I want to dance with you

Betrayed

Betrayed—by the one who says she loves you
By the one who says she needs you
Above all other men
Betrayed by her fragile, vicious beauty
Her father did his duty, and I lay down betrayed

Justice taught her competence—her mother was like steel
Her cousins, they're all convicts
She alone rose above that wheel
But a motorcyclist no matter how good
Is slave to the oncoming truck
And the poison of her father was her most pitiless luck

Three of us lie in this bed, night of infamy
One of us lies on our back, her father's in her head
And quick she turns, and slaps my face
And with her eyes open wide she screams
I hate you, I hate you, I hate you
But she's looking right past me

Betrayed—by the one who says she loves you
By the one who says that she needs you above all other men
Betrayed by her fragile, vicious beauty
Her father did his duty
And I lay down betrayed

Bottoming Out

I'm cruising fast on a motorcycle
Down this winding country road
And I pass the gravel at the foot of the hill
Where last week I fell off
There's still some oil by this old elm tree
And a dead squirrel that I hit
But if I hadn't left, I would've struck you dead
So I took a ride instead

My doctor says she hopes I know, how lucky I can be
After all it wasn't my blood mixed in the dirt that night
But this violent rage, that turns inward
Can not be helped by drink
And we must really examine this
And I say I need another drink

I'm tearing down Rte. 80 East
The sun's on my right side
I'm drunk but my vision's good
And I think of my child bride
And on the left in shadows I see
Something that makes me laugh
I aim that bike at that fat pothole beyond that underpass

Bottoming out

Home of the Brave

Here's to Johnny with his Jo and Micky's got a wife
And here's to Jerry he has got his Joyce
And me—I'm shaking
In my boots tonight
For the daughters and the sons lost in the home of the brave

Here's to the home of the brave
Here's to the life that's not saved
Here's to the home of the brave
Here's to the home of the brave

Here's to Frank hit in some bar, in picturesque Brooklyn Heights
And here's to a friend who jumped in front of a train
At seven o'clock one night
And another friend who thinks that he lacks worth
Has disappeared from sight
Somewhere in the home of the brave

The stars are hiding in their clouds
The street lights are too bright
A man's kicking a woman who's clutching his leg tight
And I think suddenly of you and blink my eyes in fright
And rush off to the home of the brave

Here's to the home of the brave
Here's to the home of the brave
Here's to the life that is saved
Here's to the home of the brave

And every day you have to die some
Cry some
Die some

Sitting in our rooftop garden
Looking down below
Sitting in our rooftop garden
Waiting for the sun
Isn't it lovely watching a plane go by
What a lovely couple are you and I

Sitting in our rooftop garden, a few drops of rain
The lights in the city blinking on
Just the same
No sugar with my coffee
How's your tea
In our rooftop garden above the city

Let's not see any letters
Let's not answer the phone
Let's just pretend that there's no one at home

In our rooftop garden
Up on the roof

LOU REED NEW SENSATIONS

I Love You, Suzanne

You broke my heart and you made me cry
You said that I couldn't dance
But now I'm back to let you know that I can really make romance

You do what you gotta do
You do everything you can
You do what you wanna do
Hey, but I love you Suzanne

You do anything once
You try anything twice
You do what you gotta do
Hey but I love you Suzanne

I love you when you're good
I love you when you're bad
You do what you gotta do
But I love you Suzanne

You do what you wanna do
You do what you can
You do what you wanna do babe
But I love you Suzanne

Endlessly Jealous

Jealousy endlessly sweeps through my mind
Jealousy often causes me to be unkind
I'm sorry I said that
I'm sorry I did that
I'm sorry I hit you
I'm sorry
I'm sorry

Endlessly jealous of you
Being endlessly jealous of me
The man that you thought I could be
Turning red with jealousy

Endlessly jealousy eats through my skull
Endlessly jealousy makes me feel dull
Fighting endless jealous fighting
I feel my fingers tightening
Tightening please don't break her arm
Jealously thinking of you
Of your endless possession of me
Of my jealousy/endlessly/jealously
Endlessly jealous of you

Sorry
Running to a phone to say
I'm sorry
Running out of dimes
The phone on the street
Spits at me—have a good day
Sorry
Please you know how I am sorry
I've been this way for oh so long
Endlessly/jealously/jealous of you

Jealousy endlessly eats through my mind
Jealousy endlessly makes me be unkind
I'm sorry I said that
I'm sorry I did that
I'm sorry I hit you
I'm sorry
I'm sorry

Endlessly jealous of you
Being endlessly jealous of me
Endlessly jealous of you
Being endlessly jealous of me

Endlessly jealous of you
Endlessly jealous of you

My Red Joystick

The first bite of the apple made Eve smart
The second bite taught her how to break men's hearts
The third bite taught her how to strut her stuff
But she never got to the fourth bite that says
Enough is enough

Enough is enough baby
I've had enough of you
You can keep your dresses
You can keep your jewels
You can keep the color TV
Those soaps just make me sick
All I'm asking you to leave me
Is my Red Joystick

My Red Joystick, my Red Joystick
All I'm asking you to leave me is my Red Joystick

Eve kissed Abel
That's how he got murdered by Cain
Abraham gave up his son
To keep his wife away
And even the Lord almighty
Speaking from the trenches to the pits
Spoke for all mankind when he said

Take the Porsche
Take the kids
Take the stocks
Baby take the rugs
Take those roses
From my poor heart wilting
But please please please
Leave me my Red Joystick

Eve drank apple cider,
Eve brewed good apple wine
Eve cooked up stewed apples
Knew how to have a good time
She came into the bedroom
Raised her skirts up high
She said, "If a little knowledge is a dangerous thing, baby,
Give me a piece before I die"

Hey Eve take a bite of my apple
I know you think you're pretty slick
The one thing I ask you to leave me
Is my Red Joystick

My Red Joystick
My Red Joystick
All I'm asking you to leave me is my Red Joystick
My Red Joystick baby
My Red Joystick
All I'm asking you to leave me is
My Red Joystick

Turn To Me

If you gave up major vices
You're between a hard place and a wall
And your car breaks down in traffic on the street
Remember, I'm the one who loves you
You can always give me a call

If your father is freebasing
And your mother turning tricks
That's still no reason you should have a rip
Remember, I'm the one who loves you
You can always give me a call

When your teeth are ground down to the bone
And there's nothing between your legs
And some friend died of something that you can't pronounce
Remember I'm the one who loves you
You can always give me a call

You can't pay your rent
Your boss is an idiot and
Your apartment has no heat and
Your wife says maybe it's time to have a child
Remember I'm the one who loves you
You can always give me a call

When it's all too much, you turn the TV set on
And light a cigarette and
Then a public service announcement
Comes creeping on and
You see a lung corroding
Or a fatal heart attack

Turn to me

New Sensations

I don't like guilt be it stoned or stupid
Drunk and disorderly I ain't no cupid
Two years ago today I was arrested on Christmas Eve
I don't want pain, I want to walk not be carried
I don't want to give it up, I want to stay married
I ain't no dog tied to a parked car

I want the principles of a timeless muse
I want to eradicate my negative views
And get rid of those people who are always on a down
It's easy enough to tell what is wrong
But that's not what I want to hear all night long
Some people are like human Tuinals

I took my GPZ out for a ride
The engine felt good between my thighs
The air felt cool it was forty degrees outside
I rode to Pennsylvania near the Delaware Gap
Sometimes I got lost and had to check the map
I stopped at a roadside diner for a burger and a Coke
There were some country folk and some hunters inside
Somebody got themselves married and somebody died
I went to the jukebox and played a hillbilly song
They was arguing about football, as I waved and went outside
And I headed for the mountains, feeling warm inside
I love that GPZ so much, you know that I could kiss her

Doin' The Things That We Want To

The other night we went to see Sam's play
(Doin' the things that we want to)
It was very physical it held you to the stage
(Doin' the things that he wants to)
The guy's a cowboy from some rodeo
(Doin' the things that he wants to)
The girl had once loved him but now she wants to go
(Doin' the things that she wants to)

The man was bullish, the woman was a tease
(Doin' the things that they want to)
They fought with their words, their bodies and their deeds
(Doin' the things that they want to)
And when they finished fighting, they exited the stage
(Doin' the things that they want to)
I was firmly struck by the way they had behaved
Doin' the things that they want to
Doin' the things that they want to

It reminds me of the movies Marty made about New York
Those frank and brutal movies that are so brilliant
Fool for Love meet The Raging Bull
They're very inspirational I love the things they do
Doin' the things that I want to

There's not much you hear on the radio today
But you can still see a movie or a play
Here's to Travis Bickle and here's to Johnny Boy
Growing up in the mean streets of New York

I wrote this song 'cause I'd like to shake your hand
In a way you guys are the best friends I ever had

What Becomes A Legend Most

What becomes a legend most—when she's alone in a hotel lobby
What becomes a legend most—some bad Champagne and some foreign bottled beer
What becomes a legend most—when the musicians have come and then leave her
What becomes a legend most—besides being a legendary star
What becomes a legend most—lying in bed cold and regal
What becomes a legend most—lying in bed watching a talk show on TV
What becomes a legend most—50 days in 50 cities and
Everyone says she looks pretty
At least as pretty as a legend should

Fifty days can wear you down
Fifty cities flying by
A different man in each different hotel
And if you're not careful word can get around

What becomes a legend most—not a bed that is half-empty
Not a heart that is left empty
That's not pretty, not pretty at all

What becomes a legend most—when she's lying in her hotel room
What becomes a legend most
Well baby tonight it's you

Fly Into The Sun

I would not run from the Holocaust
I would not run from the bomb
I'd welcome the chance to meet my maker
And fly into the sun
Fly into the sun
Fly into the sun
I'd break up into a million pieces and fly into the sun

I would not run from the blazing light
I would not run from its rain
I'd see it as an end to misery as an end to worldly pain
An end to worldly pain—an end to worldly pain
I'd shine by the light of the unknown moment
To end this worldly pain

The earth is weeping, the sky is shaking
The stars split to their core
And every proton and unnamed neutron is fusing in my bones
And an unnamed mammal is darkly rising
As man burns from his tomb
And I look at this as a blissful moment to fly into the sun
Fly into the sun—fly into the sun
I'd burn up into a million pieces and fly into the sun
To end this mystery, answer my mystery
I'd look at this as a wondrous moment to end this mystery
Fly into the sun—fly into the sun
I'd break up into a million pieces and fly into the sun

My Friend George

Read in the paper about a man killed with a sword
And that made me think of my friend George
People said the man was five foot six
Sounds like Georgie with his killing stick

I knew Georgie since he's eight
I always thought that he was great and
Anything that George would do
You know that I would do it too
George liked music and George liked to fight
He worked out in a downtown gym every night
I'd spar with him when work was done
We split lips but it was all in fun

Next thing I hear George's got this stick
He's using it for more than kicks
I seen him down at Smalley's bar
He was wired up, I tried to calm him down
Avenge yourself he says to me—avenge yourself for humanity
Avenge yourself for the weak and the poor
Stick it to these guys right through their heads
The fight is my music, the stick is my sword
And you know that I love you, so please don't say a word
Can't you hear the music playing, the anthem, it's my call
And the last I seen of Georgie was him running through the door

Hey bro, what's the word—talkin' 'bout my friend George
Hey bro, what's the word—you talkin' 'bout my friend George

High In The City

I got the time
I got my feet
Let's go hit the street
I got my mace and you got your knife
You gotta protect your own life

I wanna get high in the city
I wanna stay alive here in the city
I wanna stay high in the city
High in the city/high in the city
Let's not walk down Sutton Place
You know everybody there's gotten Akitas
Don't want to talk politics today
I feel too good
Let me have my way
Watch out for that guy on your right
Seen him on the news last Saturday night
He was high in the city
High in the city
Hey, look they're setting fire to that Jeep
There's not much you can keep
I want to stay alive in the city

So many people feeling low
And there's only one way to go to get
High in the city
High in the city
Let's grab a pie, let's hit the park
I'll kiss and hug you till it gets dark
Here in the city
Getting high in the city

Down At The Arcade

Down at the Arcade the defender is there
Down off of Broadway he's there playing his games
It's very dangerous putting money down on Robotron
Oh, I'm the Great Defender
And I really know just how to get along

A fistful of quarters, a fifty dollar stake
Life is a gamble on videotape
I called a disc jockey to dedicate a song to Blair
It's the Temps singing "I'll Be There"

The president called to give me the news
I've been awarded the Nobel Prize in Rhythm and Blues
And Stevie Wonder wants to record one of my songs
Oh, I'm the Great Defender
And I really know just how to get along

Oh, I'm the Great Defender, listen to my song
I really hope you like it, it isn't very long
It's rooted in the fifties but its heart's in 1984
And if you really like it,
Then I'll sing it for you once more

Down at the Arcade
Oh I'm the Great Defender
And I really think I've got it made

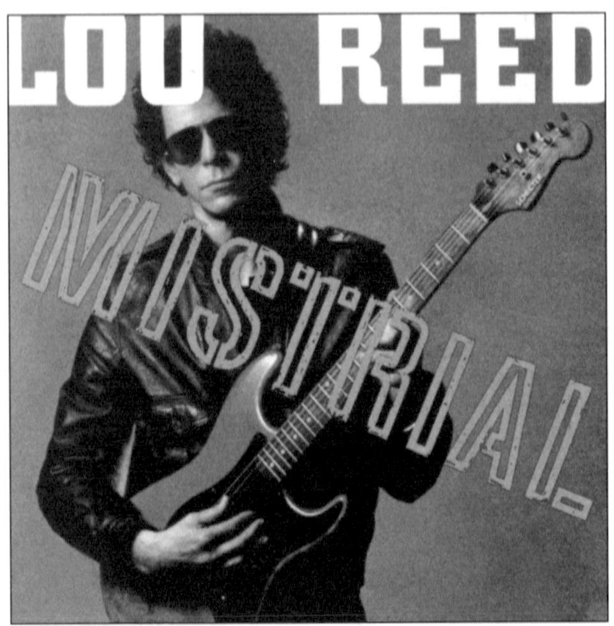
LOU REED
MISTRIAL

Mistrial

When I was six I had my first lady
When I was eight my first drink
When I was 14 I was speeding in the streets
What could anybody say to me
You can call Mister
You can call me Sir
But don't you point your finger at me

I want a Mistrial
To clear my name
I want a Mistrial in front of the people
I want a Mistrial
To clear my name
I want to bring my case to the people of New York City

When I was 30 my attitude was bad
If I said differently it'd be a lie
But there's some smarts you learn down in the street
That a college education can't buy

I want a Mistrial
To clear my name
I want a Mistrial in front of the people
I want a Mistrial
To clear my name
I want to bring my case in front of the people
of New York City

And I said M-I-S-T-R-I-A-L—Mistrial
In front of all the people

And I says M-I-S-T-R-I-A-L—Mistrial
In front of the people of New York City

No Money Down

I know you're disappointed
In the way I handled things
You're thinking I misread the times
And acted cowardly
And since what I do affects us both
And you feel that I let you down

They say there's someone for everyone
And for everyone a someone
And some tattoo roses across their chests
With a heart that says Rollo
And some work without a public relations man
And do their best work
Babe out of sight

Now I have known a hero or two
And they all learn to swim through mud
And they all got boots caked with
Dirty soles that they get from
Squashing bugs
So when push comes to shove
Get the Harley revved up
The moon can eclipse even the sun

You're paying a price
When there's no price to pay
Lovers trust—no money down
It's a lover's trust—no money down

Outside

Outside the world's a mindless child—outside
Outside reflects the worst of styles—outside
Inside when you're in my arms
A mindless child is still to be born
Inside, baby, when we come inside

Outside the politics of greed—outside
Outside misbehavior seethes—outside
Mindless repression dominates the street
While I kneel down and kiss your feet
Inside, baby, when we come inside—outside

Outside they don't think, they breed—outside
Outside emotion determines need—outside
Outside the world's a mindless child
That we could bring to life
In your arms
Inside, baby, when we come inside

Outside the politics of hate and greed—outside
Outside the world's a mindless child—outside
But when I hold you in my arms
It's a mindless child that you want
Inside, no matter 'bout the world outside
Inside, a baby's what you want inside

Don't Hurt a Woman

I was angry
I said things I shouldn't say
But please don't turn your back

Sometimes I get so upset
But I take it all back

Please don't go
I know I was wrong
Sometimes—I don't know
What comes over me

But I try to remember
Don't hurt a woman

I was angry
I said things I shouldn't say
I must have lost control
Sometimes something clicks in my head
And I'm not myself anymore

That wasn't me
You can't believe everything you see
Let's make believe I never said a word
And I'll try to remember
Don't hurt a woman

Video Violence

The currents rage deep inside us
This is the age of video violence
The currents rage so deep inside us
This is the age of video violence

Up in the morning, drinking his coffee
Turns on the TV to some slasher movie
Cartoon-like women, tied up and sweaty
Panting and screaming
Thank you, have a nice day

His heart is pounding he switches the channel
Looking for something other than rape or murder
Or beatings or torture
But except for Walt Disney
It's a twisted alliance
This age of video violence

Down at his job his boss sits there screaming
If he loses his job, then life loses its meaning
His son is in high school
There's nothing he's learning
He sits by the TV
Watching Corvettes exploding 'cause

Down at a bar some woman is topless
She's acned and scarred, her hair is a mess
While he shoves $5 down her exotic panties
The video jukebox is playing Madonna

While just down the block
At some local theater
They're grabbing their crotches
At the 13th beheading
As the dead rise to live
The live sink to die
The currents are deep and raging inside

Our good working stiff looks a whore in the eye
Ties her to a bed
While he beats her back bloody
And then back at home
Drinking more instant coffee
Calls some red-neck evangelist that
He's seen on TV and says

The currents rage, the dawn's upon us
This is the age of video violence
No age of reason is landing upon us
This is the age of video violence

The currents rage so deep within us
This is the age of video violence
The currents rage so deep down inside us
This is the age of video violence

Spit It Out

If there's rage inside you
So you cannot think
Spit it out
If you get so angry
That you cannot speak
Spit it out

Talk to him or her or it
And tell them where they can put it
Spit it out
Spit it out
You got to talk to him or her or it
And take aim with your mouth and spit
Spit it out
Spit it out

If you get worked over at your job
Spit it out
If a taxi almost runs you down
Spit it out
You got to take aim with your mouth
And speak and give it to them right between the teeth
Spit it out
Spit it out

Talk to him or her or it
And take aim with your mouth and spit
Spit it out
Spit it out

If you're patient and you have the time
Spit it out
Wait till they're on the decline
Spit it out
The Chinese say you meet the hard with the soft
The Yin with the Yang
The down with the up
Spit it out
Spit it out
You got to grab that dumb he, she or it
And give it to them right between the teeth
Spit it out
Spit it out

The Original Wrapper

I was sittin' home on the West End
Watchin' cable TV with a female friend
We were watchin' the news, the world's in a mess
The poor and the hungry, a world in distress
Herpes, AIDS, the Middle East at full throttle
Better check that sausage before you put it in the waffle
And while you're at it—check what's in the batter
Make sure the candy's in the
Original Wrapper

Reagan says abortion's murder
While he's looking at Cardinal O'Connor
Look at Jerry Falwell, Louis Farrakhan
Both talk religion and the brotherhood of man
They both sound like they belong in Teheran
Watch out, they're goin' full throttle
Better watch that sausage before you put it in the waffle
And while you're at it—better check that batter
Make sure the candy's in the
Original Wrapper
Hey, pitcher, better check that batter
Make sure the candy's in the
Original Wrapper

White against white, Black against Jew
It seems like it's 1942
The baby sits in front of MTV watching violent fantasies
While Dad guzzles beer with his favorite sport
Only to find his heroes are all coked up
It's classic, original—the same old story
The politics of hate in a new surrounding
Hate if it's good and hate if it's bad
And if this all don't make you mad
I'll keep yours and I'll keep mine
Nothing sacred and nothing divine
Father, bless me—we're going full throttle
Better check that sausage before you put it in the waffle
And while you're at it better check that batter
Make sure the candy's in the Original Wrapper

I was born in the United States
I grew up hard but I grew up straight
I saw a lack of morals and a lack of concern
A feeling that there's nowhere to turn
Yippies, Hippies and upwardly mobile Yuppies
Don't treat me like I'm some damn lackey
'Cause the murderer lives while the victims die,
I'd much rather see it an eye for an eye
A heart for a heart, a brain for a brain
And if this all makes you feel a little insane
Kick up your heels—turn the music up loud
Pick up your guitar and look out at the crowd
And say, "Don't mean to come on sanctimonious
But life's got me nervous and a little pugnacious-
Lugubrious so I give a salutation
And rock on out to beat really fabulous
Ohh poop ah doo and how do you do
Hip hop gonna bop till I drop."
Watch out world, comin' at you full throttle
Better check that sausage before you put it in the waffle
And while you're at it, better check that batter
Make sure the candy's in the Original Wrapper
Hey, hey pitcher better check that batter
Make sure the candy's in the
Original Wrapper

Mama's Got a Lover

Mama's got a Lover
A painter I am told
She's getting out of real estate
For the art scene down in old Soho

Mama's got a Lover
He owns a gallery
She says he likes collages but
The money's in GRA-FI-TI

Mama's got a Lover
I met him yesterday
She says she hopes I like him
Maybe I'll send him a card on Father's Day

Mama's got a Lover
They're backing a film
It's about a working mother
Who gives birth to black and white
Siamese twins

Mama's got a Lover
He's got something to say
He says he's into dirt and rot
The essence of "urban decay"

Mama's got a Lover
We met yesterday
She says she hopes I like him
I'll send him a card on Father's Day

Mama's got a Lover
I met him yesterday
She's starting a new chapter
I wish she was on the last page

I Remember You

I remember you, I remember me
I remember, I remember how things used to be
I remember every word that you said
I remember, how could I forget
Yes, I remember, I remember you

I remember you, I remember your old address and
I remember, how could I forget
I remember thinking how my luck changed
I remember being so amazed
I remember, I remember you

I remember you, I remember me
I remember the way things used to be
I remember how it was that we met
I remember, I will never forget 'cause
I remember, I remember you

Tell It To Your Heart

I'm staring through a telescope at night
At a large light in the sky—
Its spinning lights reminded me of you
A star spinning in orbit lighting up the sky
Or maybe it was not a star at all

I'm standing by the Hudson River's edge at night
Looking out across the Jersey shore
At a neon light spelling out some cola's name
And I thought
Your name should be dancing beamed from satellites
Larger than any billboard in Times Square

Tell it to your heart
Please don't be afraid
I'm the one who loves you in each and every way
Tell it to your heart
Please don't be afraid
New York City lovers
Tell it to your heart

I'm up on the roof, it's 5 A.M., I guess I couldn't sleep
And I see this spinning light that I saw last week
Maybe I should wake you up but by then it might be gone
You never know what you see when you look up in the sky

I ran outside down a darkened street listening
To my boot heels click
My leather jacket squeaked, I needed a cigarette
When I turned the corner my spinning light was in the street
They were filming a commercial on TV

Tell it to your heart
Please don't be afraid
We're no teenage movie
That ends in tragedy
Tell it to your heart
Please don't be afraid
New York City lovers
Tell it to your heart

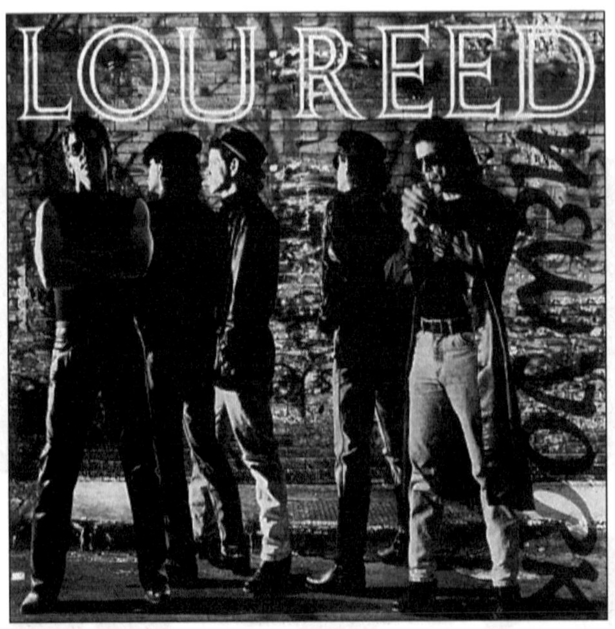
LOU REED
NEW YORK

Romeo Had Juliette

Caught between the twisted stars the plotted lines the faulty map
That brought Columbus to New York
Betwixt between the East and West
He calls on her wearing a leather vest
The earth squeals and shudders to a halt
A diamond crucifix in his ear is used to help ward off the fear
That he has left his soul in someone's rented car
Inside his pants he hides a mop to clean the mess that he has dropped
Into the life of lithesome Juliette Bell

And Romeo wanted Juliette
And Juliette wanted Romeo

Romeo Rodriguez squares his shoulders and curses Jesus
Runs a comb through his black pony-tail
He's thinking of his lonely room
The sink that by his bed gives off a stink
Then smells her perfume in his eyes
And her voice was like a bell

Outside the streets were steaming the crack dealers were dreaming
Of an Uzi someone had just scored
I betcha I could hit that light with my one good arm behind my back
Says little Joey Diaz
Brother, give me another tote
Those downtown hoods are no damn good
Those Italians need a lesson to be taught

This cop who died in Harlem, you think they'd get the warnin'
I was dancing when I saw his brains run out on the street

And Romeo had Juliette
And Juliette had her Romeo

I'll take Manhattan in a garbage bag with Latin written on it that says
"It's hard to give a shit these days"
Manhattan's sinking like a rock, into the filthy Hudson what a shock
They wrote a book about it, they said it was like Ancient Rome
The perfume burned his eyes, holding tightly to her thighs
And something flickered for a minute
And then it vanished and was gone

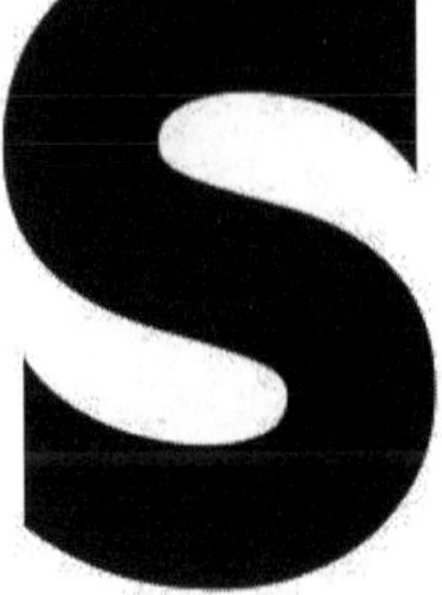

Halloween Parade

There's a downtown fairy singing out "Proud Mary"
As she cruises Christopher Street
And some southern queen is acting loud and mean
Where the docks and the badlands meet
This Halloween is something to be sure
Especially to be here without you

There's a Greta Garbo and an Alfred Hitchcock
And some black Jamaican stud
There's five Cinderellas and some leather drags
I almost fell into my mug
There's a Crawford, Davis and a tacky Cary Grant
And some homeboys lookin' for trouble down here from the Bronx

But there ain't no Hairy and no Virgin Mary
You won't hear those voices again
And Johnny Rio and Rotten Rita
You'll never see those faces again
This Halloween is something to be sure
Especially to be here without you

There's the Born Again Losers and the Lavender Boozers
And some crack team from Washington Heights
The boys from Avenue B, the girls from Avenue D
A Tinkerbell in tights
This celebration somehow gets me down
Especially when I see you're not around

There's no Peter Pedantic saying things romantic
In Latin, Greek or Spic
There's no Three Bananas or Brandy Alexander
Dishing all their tricks

It's a different feeling that I have today
Especially when I know you've gone away
There's a girl from Soho with a teeshirt saying, "I blow"
She's with the "Jive Five 2 Plus 3"
And the girls for pay dates are giving cut rates
Or else doing it for free
The past keeps knock knock knocking on my door
And I don't want to hear it anymore
No consolations please
For feelin' funky
I got to get my head above my knees
But it makes me mad and mad makes me sad
And then I start to freeze
In the back of my mind I was afraid it might be true
In the back of my mind I was afraid that they meant you
The Halloween Parade
See you next year—
At the Halloween Parade

Dirty Blvd.

Pedro lives out of the Wilshire Hotel
He looks out a window without glass
The walls are made of cardboard
Newspapers on his feet
And his father beats him 'cause he's too tired to beg
He's got nine brothers and sisters
They're brought up on their knees
It's hard to run when a coat hanger beats you on the thighs
Pedro dreams of being older and killing the old man
But that's a slim chance he's going to the boulevard

This room cost $2,000 a month
You can believe it man it's true
Somewhere a landlord's laughing till he wets his pants
No one here dreams of being a doctor or a lawyer or anything
They dream of dealing on the dirty boulevard

Give me your hungry, your tired, your poor I'll piss on 'em
That's what the Statue of Bigotry says
Your poor huddled masses—lets club 'em to death
And get it over with and just dump 'em on the boulevard

Outside it's a bright night, there's an opera at Lincoln Center
And movie stars arrive by limousine
The klieg lights shoot up over the skyline of Manhattan
But the lights are out on the mean streets

A small kid stands by the Lincoln Tunnel
He's selling plastic roses for a buck
The traffic's backed up to 39th Street
The TV whores are calling the cops out for a suck

And back at the Wilshire, Pedro sits there dreaming
He's found a book on magic in a garbage can
He looks at the pictures and stares up at the cracked ceiling
"At the count of three," he says, "I hope I can disappear
and fly fly away . . ."

Endless Cycle

The bias of the father runs on through the son
Leaving him bothered and bewildered
The drugs in his veins only cause him to spit
At the face staring back in the mirror
How can he tell a good act from the bad
He can't even remember his name
How can he do what needs to be done
When he's a follower and not a leader
The sickness of the mother runs on through the girl
Leaving her small and helpless
Liquor flies through her brain with the force of a gun
Leaving her running in circles
How can she tell a good act from the bad
When she's flat on her back in her room
How can she do what needs to be done
When she's a coward and a bleeder
The man if he marries will batter his child
And have endless excuses
The woman sadly will do much the same
Thinking that it's right and it's proper
Better than their mommy or their daddy did
Better than the childhood they suffered
The truth is they're happier when they're in pain
In fact, that's why they got married

There Is No Time

This is no time for celebration
This is no time for shaking hands
This is no time for back-slapping
This is no time for marching bands
This is no time for optimism
This is no time for endless thought
This is no time for my country right or wrong
Remember what that brought

There is no time

This is no time for congratulations
This is no time to turn your back
This is no time for circumlocution
This is no time for learned speech
This is no time to count your blessings
This is no time for private gain
This is a time to put up or shut up
It won't come back this way again

There is no time

This is no time to swallow anger
This is no time to ignore hate
This is no time be acting frivolous
Because the time is getting late
This is no time for private vendettas
This is no time to not know who you are
Self-knowledge is a dangerous thing
The freedom of who you are
This is no time to ignore warnings
This is no time to clear the plate
Let's not be sorry after the fact
And let the past become our fate

There is no time

This is no time to turn away and drink
Or smoke some vials of crack
This is a time to gather force
And take dead aim and attack
This is no time for celebration
This is no time for saluting flags
This is no time for inner searchings
The future is at hand
This is no time for phony rhetoric
This is no time for political speech
This is a time for action
Because the future's within reach

This is the time, because there is no time

Last Great American Whale

They say he didn't have an enemy
His was a greatness to behold
He was the last surviving progeny
The last one on this side of the world
He measured a half mile from tip to tail
Silver and black with powerful fins
They say he could split a mountain in two
That's how we got the Grand Canyon

Some say they saw him at the Great Lakes
Some say they saw him off of Florida
My mother said she saw him in Chinatown
But you can't always trust your mother
Off the Carolinas the sun shines brightly in the day
The lighthouse glows ghostly there at night
The chief of a local tribe had killed a racist mayor's son
And he'd been on death row since 1958
The mayor's kid was a rowdy pig
Spit on Indians and lots worse
The Old Chief buried a hatchet in his head
Life compared to death for him seemed worse
The tribal brothers gathered in the lighthouse to sing
And tried to conjure up a storm or rain
The harbor parted and the great whale sprang full up
And caused a huge tidal wave
The wave crushed the jail and freed the chief
The tribe let out a roar
The whites were drowned
The browns and reds set free

But sadly one thing more
Some local yokel member of the NRA
Kept a bazooka in his living room
And thinking he had the Chief in his sights
Blew the whale's brains out with a lead harpoon

Well Americans don't care for much of anything
Land and water the least
And animal life is low on the totem pole
With human life not worth more than infected yeast
Americans don't care too much for beauty
They'll shit in a river, dump battery acid in a stream
They'll watch dead rats wash up on the beach
And complain if they can't swim
They say things are done for the majority
Don't believe half of what you see
And none of what you hear

It's like what my painter friend Donald said to me,
"Stick a fork in their ass and turn them over, they're sick"

Beginning of a Great Adventure

It might be fun to have a kid that I could kick around
A little me to fill up with my thoughts
A little me or he or she to fill up with my dreams
A way of saying life is not a loss
I'd keep the tyke away from school
And tutor him myself
Keep him from the poison of the crowd
But then again pristine isolation
Might not be the best idea
It's not good trying to immortalize yourself

Why stop at one, I might have ten, a regular TV brood
I'd breed a little liberal army in the woods
Just like these redneck lunatics I see at the local bar
With their tribe of mutant inbred piglets with cloven hooves
I'd teach 'em how to plant a bomb, start a fire, play guitar
And if they catch a hunter, shoot him in the nuts
I'd try to be as progressive as I could possibly be
As long as I don't have to try too much

Susie, Jesus, Bogart, Sam, Leslie, Jill and Jeff
Rita, Winny, Andy, Fran and Jet
Boris, Bono, Lucy, Ethel, Bunny, Reg and Tom
That's a lot of names to try not to forget
Carrie, Marlon, Mo and Steve
La Rue and Jerry Lee
Eggplant, Rufus, Dummy, Star and The Glob
I'd need a damn computer to keep track of all these names
I hope this baby thing don't go too far

I hope it's true what my wife said to me
She says, baby, "It's the beginning of a great adventure"

It might be fun to have a kid that I could kick around
Create in my own image like a god
I'd raise my own pallbearers to carry me to the grave
And keep me company when I'm a wizened toothless clod
Some gibbering old fool sitting all alone drooling on his shirt
Some senile old fart playing in the dirt
It might be fun to have a kid I could pass something on to
Something better than rage, pain, anger and hurt

Busload of Faith

You can't depend on your family
You can't depend on your friends
You can't depend on a beginning
You can't depend on an end
You can't depend on intelligence
You can't depend on God
You can only depend on one thing
You need a busload of faith to get by

You can depend on the worst always happening
You can depend on a murderer's drive
You can bet that if he rapes somebody
There'll be no trouble having a child
And you can bet that if she aborts it
Pro-lifers will attack her with rage
You can depend on the worst always happening
You need a busload of faith to get by

You can't depend on the goodly-hearted
The goodly-hearted made lampshades and soap
You can't depend on the Sacrament
No Father, no Holy Ghost
You can't depend on any churches
Unless there's real estate that you want to buy
You can't depend on a lot of things
You need a busload of faith to get by

You can't depend on no miracle
You can't depend on the air
You can't depend on a wise man
You can't find them because they're not there
You can depend on cruelty
Crudity of thought and sound
You can depend on the worst always happening
YOU NEED
A BUSLOAD
OF FAITH
TO GET BY

Sick of You

I was up in the morning with the TV blarin'
Brushed my teeth sittin' watchin' the news
All the beaches were closed the ocean was a Red Sea
But there was no one there to part it in two
There was no fresh salad 'cause
There's hypos in the cabbage
Staten Island disappeared at noon
And they say the Midwest is in great distress
And NASA blew up the moon
The ozone layer has no ozone anymore
And you're gonna leave me for the guy next door
I'm sick of you

They arrested the mayor for an illegal favor
Sold the Empire State to Japan
And Oliver North married Richard Secord
And gave birth to a little Teheran
And the Ayatollah bought a nuclear warship
If he dies he wants to go out in style
And there's nothing to eat that don't carry the stink
Of some human waste dumped in the Nile
Well one thing is certainly true
No one here knows what to do
And I'm sick of you

The radio said there were 400 dead
In some small town in Arkansas
Some whacked-out trucker
Drove into a nuclear reactor

And killed everybody he saw
Now he's on Morton Downey
And he's glowing and shining
Doctors say this is a medical advance
They say the bad makes the good
And there's something to be learned
In every human experience
Well I know one thing that really is true
This here's a zoo and the keeper ain't you
And I'm sick of it, I'm sick of you
They ordained the Trumps and then he got the mumps
And died being treated at Mt. Sinai
And my best friend Bill died from a poison pill
Some wired doctor prescribed for stress
My arms and legs are shrunk
The food all has lumps
They discovered some animal no one's ever seen
It was an inside trader eating a rubber tire
After running over Rudy Giuliani
They say the president's dead
No one can find his head
It's been missing now for weeks
But no one noticed it
He had seemed so fit
And I'm sick of it
I'm sick of you
Bye, bye, bye

Hold On

There's blacks with knives and whites with clubs
Fighting at Howard Beach
There's no such thing as human rights
When you walk the N.Y. streets
A cop was shot in the head by a 10-year-old kid named Buddah
In Central Park last week
The fathers and daughters are lined up by
The coffins by the Statue of Bigotry

You better hold on—something's happening here
You better hold on—well I'll meet you in Tompkins Square

The dopers sent a message to the cops last weekend
They shot him in the car where he sat
And Eleanor Bumpers and Michael Stewart must have
appreciated that
There's a rampaging rage rising up like a plague of bloody vials
Washing up on the beach
It'll take more than the Angels or Iron Mike Tyson
To heal this bloody breach

A junkie ran down a lady, a pregnant dancer
She'll never dance but the baby was saved
He shot up some China White and nodded out at the wheel
And he doesn't remember a thing
They shot that old lady 'cause they thought she was a witness
To a crime she didn't even see
Whose home is the home of the brave by the Statue of Bigotry

You got a black .38 and a gravity knife
You still have to ride the train
There's the smelly essence of N.Y. down there
But you ain't no Bernard Goetz
There's no mafia lawyer to fight in your corner
For that 15 minutes of fame
The have and havenots are bleeding in the tub
That's New York's future not mine

Good Evening Mr. Waldheim

Good evening, Mr. Waldheim
And Pontiff how are you?
You have so much in common
In the things you do
And here comes Jesse Jackson
He talks of common ground
Does that common ground include me
Or is it just a sound
A sound that shakes
Oh Jesse, you must watch the sounds you make
A sound that quakes
There are fears that still reverberate

Jesse you say common ground
Does that include the PLO?
What about people right here right now
Who fought for you not so long ago?
The words that flow so freely
Falling dancing from your lips
I hope that you don't cheapen them with a racist slip
Oh common ground
Is common ground a word or just a sound
Common ground—remember those civil rights workers
buried in the ground

If I ran for president and once was a member of the Klan
Wouldn't you call me on it
The way I call you on Farrakhan
And Pontiff, pretty Pontiff
Can anyone shake your hand?
Or is it just that you like uniforms and someone kissing your hand
Or is it true
The common ground for me includes you, too

Good evening, Mr. Waldheim
Pontiff how are you
As you both stroll through the woods at night
I'm thinking thoughts of you
And Jesse you're inside my thoughts
As the rhythmic words subside
My common ground invites you in
Or do you prefer to wait outside
Or is it true
The common ground for me is without you
Or is it true
There's no ground common enough for me and you

GOOD EVENING, MR. WALDHEIM
PONTIFF HOW ARE YOU
AS YOU BOTH STROLL THROUGH THE WOODS AT NIGHT
I'M THINKING THOUGHTS OF YOU
AND JESSE YOU'RE INSIDE MY THOUGHTS

Xmas in February

Sam was lyin' in the jungle
Agent Orange spread against the sky like marmalade
Hendrix played on some foreign jukebox
They were praying to be saved
Those Gooks were fierce and fearless
That's the price you pay when you invade
Xmas in February

Sam lost his arm in some border town
His fingers are mixed with someone's crop
If he didn't have that opium to smoke
The pain would never ever stop
Half his friends are stuffed into black body bags
With their names printed at the top
Xmas in February

Sammy was a short-order cook in a
Short-order black and blue collar town
Everybody worked the steel mill but
The steel mill got closed down
He thought if he joined the Army
He'd have a future that was sound
Like no Xmas in February

Sam's staring at the Vietnam wall
It's been a while now that he's home
His wife and kid have left, he's unemployed
He's a reminder of the war that wasn't won
He's that guy on the street with the sign that reads
"Please help send this Vet home"
But he is home
And there's no Xmas in February
No matter how much he saves

Strawman

We who have so much
To you who have so little
To you who don't have anything at all
We who have so much
More than any one man does need
And you who don't have anything at all
Does anybody need another million dollar movie
Does anybody need another million dollar star
Does anybody need to be told over and over
Spitting in the wind comes back at you twice as hard

Strawman, going straight to the devil
Strawman, going straight to hell

Does anyone really need a billion dollar rocket
Does anyone need a $60,000 car
Does anyone need another president
Or the sins of Swaggart, parts 6, 7, 8 and 9
Does anyone need yet another politician
Caught with his pants down
Money sticking in his hole
Does anyone need another racist preacher
Spittin' in the wind can only do you harm

Does anyone need another faulty shuttle
Blasting off to the moon, Venus or Mars
Does anybody need another self-righteous rock singer
Whose nose he says led him straight to God
Does anyone need yet another blank skyscraper
If you're like me I'm sure a minor miracle will do
A flaming sword or maybe a gold ark floating up the Hudson
When you spit in the wind it comes right back at you

Dime Store Mystery

He was lying banged and battered, skewered
And bleeding, talking crippled on the cross
Was his mind reeling and heaving
Hallucinating fleeing what a loss
The things he hadn't touched or kissed
His senses slowly stripped away
Not like Buddha not like Vishnu
Life wouldn't rise through him again
I find it easy to believe
That he might question his beliefs
The beginning of the last temptation
Dime store mystery

The duality of nature, godly nature, human nature
Splits the soul
Fully human, fully divine and divided
The great immortal soul
Split into pieces, whirling pieces, opposites attract
From the front, the side, the back
The mind itself attacks
I know this feeling, I know it from before
Descartes through Hegel
Belief is never sure
Dime store mystery, last temptation

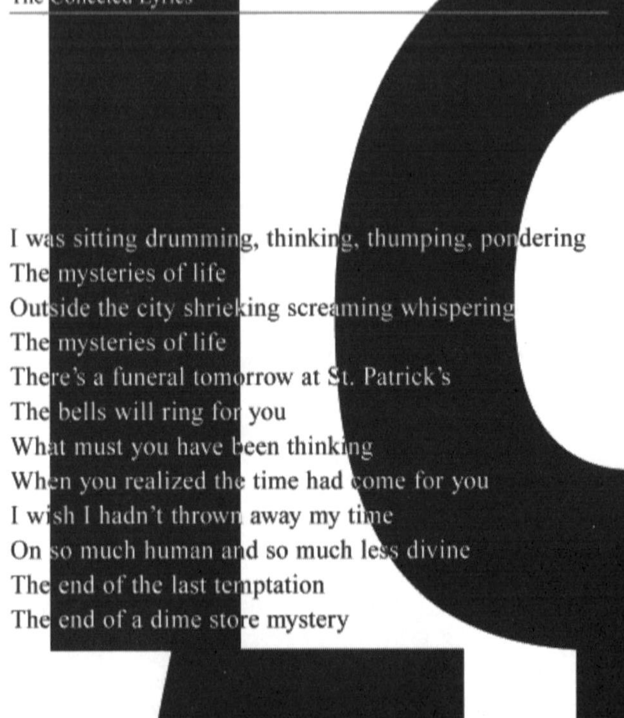

I was sitting drumming, thinking, thumping, pondering
The mysteries of life
Outside the city shrieking screaming whispering
The mysteries of life
There's a funeral tomorrow at St. Patrick's
The bells will ring for you
What must you have been thinking
When you realized the time had come for you
I wish I hadn't thrown away my time
On so much human and so much less divine
The end of the last temptation
The end of a dime store mystery

LOU REED / JOHN CALE
SONGS FOR DRELLA

Small Town

When you're growing up in a small town
When you're growing up in a small town
When you're growing up in a small town
You say no one famous ever came from here
When you're growing up in a small town
And you're having a nervous breakdown
And you think that you'll never escape it
Yourself or the place that you live
Where did Picasso come from
There's no Michelangelo coming from Pittsburgh
If art is the tip of the iceberg
I'm the part sinking below

When you're growing up in a small town
Bad skin, bad eyes—gay and fatty
People look at you funny
When you're in a small town
My father worked in construction
It's not something for which I am suited
Oh—what is something for which you are suited?
Getting out of here

I hate being odd in a small town
If they stare let them stare in New York City
At this pink-eyed painting albino
How far can my fantasy go?
I'm no Dali coming from Pittsburgh
No adorable lisping Capote
My hero—oh do you think I could meet him?
I'd camp out at his front door.

There's only one good thing about a small town
There's only one good use for a small town
There's only one good thing about a small town
You know that you want to get out

When you're growing up in a small town
You know you'll grow down in a small town
There's only one good use for a small town
You hate it and you know you'll have to leave

get out
get out
get out
get out
get out
get out
get out
get out
get out
get out
get out
get out
get out
get out
get out
get out
get out
get out
get out
get out
get out
get out

Open House

Please
Come over to 81st street I'm in the apartment above the bar
You know you can't miss it, it's across from the subway
And the tacky store with the Mylar scarves

My skin's as pale as the outdoors moon
My hair's silver like a Tiffany watch
I like lots of people around me but don't kiss hello
And please don't touch

It's a Czechoslovakian custom my mother passed on to me
The way to make friends Andy is invite them up for tea
Open house, open house

I've got a lot of cats, here's my favorite
She's a lady called Sam
I made a paper doll of her—you can have it
That's what I did when I had St. Vitus' dance
It's a Czechoslovakian custom my mother passed on to me
Give people little presents so they'll remember me
Open house, open house

Someone bring vegetables, someone please bring heat
My mother showed up yesterday, we need something to eat
I think I got a job today they want me to draw shoes
The ones I drew were old and used
They told me—draw something new
Open house, open house

Fly me to the moon, fly me to a star
But there're no stars in the New York sky
They're all on the ground
You scared yourself with music, I scared myself with paint
I drew 550 different shoes today
It almost made me faint
Open house, open house

invite them up

invite them up

invite them up

invite them up

invite them up

invite them up

the style the style the style the style the style the style the s

Style It Takes

You've got the money, I've got the time
You want your freedom, make your freedom mine
'Cause I've got the style it takes
And money is all that it takes
You've got connections and I've got the art
You like attention and I like your looks
And I have the style it takes
And you know the people it takes
Why don't you sit right over there, we'll do a movie portrait
I'll turn the camera on—and I won't even be there
A portrait that moves, you look great I think.
I'll put the Empire State Building on your wall
For 24 hours glowing on your wall
Watch the sun rise above it in your room
Wallpaper art, a great view
I've got a Brillo box and I say it's art
It's the same one you can buy at any supermarket
'Cause I've got the style it takes
And you've got the people it takes
This is a rock group called the Velvet Underground
I show movies on them
Do you like their sound
'Cause they have a style that grates and I have art to make
Let's do a movie here next week
We don't have sound but you're so great
You don't have to speak
You've got the style it takes (kiss)
You've got the style it takes (eat)
You've got the style it takes (couch)
You've got the style it takes (kiss)

tyle the style the style the style the style the style the style

Work

Andy was a Catholic, the ethic ran through his bones
He lived alone with his mother, collecting gossip and toys
Every Sunday when he went to church
He'd kneel in his pew and he'd say
"It's work, all that matters is work."

He was a lot of things, what I remember the most
He'd say, "I've got to bring home the bacon, someone's got to
  bring home the roast"
He'd get to the Factory early
If you'd ask him he'd a told you straight out
"It's work"

No matter what I did it never seemed enough
He said I was lazy, I said I was young
He said, "How many songs did you write?"
I'd written zero, I lied and said, "Ten"
"You won't be young forever—you should have written fifteen"
It's work

"You ought to make things big
People like it that way
And the songs with the dirty words make sure
  you record them that way"
Andy liked to stir up trouble, he was funny that way
He said, "It's just work"

Andy sat down to talk one day
He said, "Decide what you want"

"Do you want to expand your parameters
Or play the museums like some dilettante"
I fired him on the spot, he got red and he called me a rat
It was the worst word that he could think of
I'd never seen him like that
It was work, I thought he said it's just work

Andy said a lot of things, I stored them all away in my head
Sometimes when I can't decide what I should do
I think what would Andy have said
He'd probably say
"You think too much—That's 'cause there's work
  that you don't want to do"
It's work, the most important thing is work
It's work, the most important thing is work

"It's just work" just work"
"It's just work" just work"
"It's just work" just work"
"It's just work" just work"

Trouble with Classicists

The trouble with a classicist—he looks at a tree
That's all he sees, he paints a tree
The trouble with a classicist, he looks at the sky
He doesn't ask why, he just paints a sky

The trouble with an impressionist, he looks at a log
He doesn't know who he is, standing, staring at this log
And surrealist memories are too amorphous and proud
While those downtown macho painters are just alcoholic
The trouble with impressionists
That's the trouble with impressionists

The trouble with personalities, they're too wrapped up in style
It's too personal, they're in love with their own guile
They're like illegal aliens trying to make a buck
They're driving gypsy cabs but they're thinking like a truck
That's the trouble with personalities

I like the druggy downtown kids who spray-paint walls and trains
I like their lack of training, their primitive technique
I think sometimes it hurts you when you stay too long in school
I think sometimes it hurts you when you're afraid to be called a fool
That's the trouble with classicists

Starlight

Starlight open wide, starlight open up your door
This is New York calling, with movies from the street
Movies with real people, what you get is what you see
Starlight open wide, Andy's Cecil B. DeMille
Come on L.A. give us a call
We've got Superstars who talk, they'll do anything at all
Ingrid, Viva, Little Joe, Baby Jane, and Edie S.
But you'd better call us soon before we talk ourselves to death

Starlight open wide, everybody is a star
Split-screen eight hour movies
We've got color, we've got sound
Won't you recognize us, we're everything you hate
Andy loves old Hollywood movies, he'll scare you hypocrites to death
You know that shooting up's for real
That person who's screaming, that's the way it really feels
We're all improvising five movies in a week
If Hollywood doesn't call us—we'll be sick

Starlight open wide
Do to movies what you did to art
Can you see beauty in ugliness, or is it playing in the dirt
There are stars out on the New York streets
We're going to capture them on film
But if no one wants to see 'em
We'll make another and another

Starlight let us in that magic room
We've all dreamt of Hollywood, it can't happen too soon
Won't you give us a million dollars the rent's due
Andy'll give you two movies and a painting
Starlight open wide!

Faces and Names

Faces and names, I wish they were the same
Faces and names only cause trouble for me
Faces and names
If we all looked the same and we all had the same name
I wouldn't be jealous of you or you jealous of me
Faces and names

I always fall in love with someone who looks
The way I wish that I could be
I'm always staring at someone who hurts
And the one they really hurt is me
Faces and names, to me they're all the same
If I looked like you and you looked like me
There'd be less trouble you'd see
Faces and names I wish they'd go away
I'd disappear into that wall and never talk
Talk not talk

I wish I was a robot or a machine
Without a feeling or a thought
People who want to meet the name I have
Are always disappointed in me
Faces and names I wish they were the same
Faces and names only cause problems for me
Faces and names
I'd rather be a hole in the wall—looking on the other side
I'd rather look and listen, listen not talk
To faces and names
If I had a breakdown when I was a kid

If I lost my hair when I was young
If you dress older when you are not
As you really age, you look the same
If we all looked the same, we wouldn't play these games
Me dressing for you, you dressing for me—undressing for me

Faces and names if they all were the same
You wouldn't be jealous of me or me jealous of you
Me jealous of you—me jealous of you
Your face and your name
Your face and your name
Faces and names
Faces and names

meaning
meaning
meaning
meaning
meaning
meaning
meaning
meaning
meaning
meaning
meaning

Images

I think images are worth repeating
Images repeated from a painting
Images taken from a painting
From a photo worth re-seeing
I love images worth repeating, project them upon the ceiling
Multiply them with silk screening
See them with a different feeling
Images/those images/images/those images

Some say images have no feeling, I think there's a deeper meaning
Mechanical precision or so it's seeming
Instigates a cooler feeling
I love multiplicity of screenings
Things born anew display new meanings
I think images are worth repeating and repeating and repeating
Images/oh images/those images/images

I'm no urban idiot savant spewing paint without any order
I'm no sphinx, no mystery enigma
What I paint is very ordinary
I don't think I'm old or modern, I don't think I think I'm thinking
It doesn't matter what I am thinking
It's images are worth repeating and repeating
Those images/images/

If you're looking for a deeper meaning, I'm as deep as this
High ceiling
If you think technique is meaning, you might find me very simple
You might think the images are boring
Cars and cans and chairs and flowers
And you might find me personally boring
Hammer, sickle, Mao Tse Tung, Mao Tse Tung
Those images/those images/images

I think that it bears repeating the images upon the ceiling
I love images worth repeating and repeating and repeating
Images/images/those images/those images

Watch out	Watch out	Watch out	Watch out
Watch out	Watch out	Watch out	Watch out
Watch out	Watch out	Watch out	Watch out
Watch out	Watch out	Watch out	images
Watch out	Watch out	Watch out	Watch out
Watch out	Watch out	Watch out	Watch out
Watch out	Watch out	Watch out	Watch out
Watch out	Watch out	Watch out	Watch out

Slip Away (A Warning)

Friends have said to lock the door and have an open house no more
They said the Factory must change and slowly slip away
But if I have to live in fear, where will I get my ideas
With all those crazy people gone, will I slowly slip away

Still there's no more Billy Name, Ondine is not the same
Wonton and the Turtle gone
Slowly slip away . . . slowly slip away

If I close the Factory door and don't see those people anymore
If I give in to infamy . . . I'll slowly slip away

I know it seems that friends are right
Hello daylight, goodbye night
But starlight is so quiet here, think I'll slowly slip away

What can I do by myself, it's good to hear from someone else
It's good to hear a crazy voice—will not slip away
Will not slip away

If I have to live in fear my ideas will slowly slip away
If I have to live in fear I'm afraid my life will slip away
If you can't see me past my door
Why your thoughts could slowly slip away
If I have to lock the door, another life exists no more
Slip away

Friends have said to lock the door
Watch out for what comes through that door
They said the Factory must change
But I don't

It Wasn't Me

It wasn't me who shamed you, it's not fair to say that
You wanted to work—I gave you a chance at that
It wasn't me who hurt you, that's more credit than I'm worth
Don't threaten me with the things you do to you

It wasn't me who shamed you, it wasn't me who brought
You down
You did it to yourself without any help from me
It wasn't me who hurt you, I showed you possibilities
The problems you had were there before you met me

I didn't say this had to be
You can't blame these things on me
It wasn't me, it wasn't me, it wasn't me
I know she's dead, it wasn't me

It wasn't me who changed you, you did it to yourself
I'm not an excuse for the hole that you dropped in
I'm not simpleminded but I'm no father to you all
Death exists but you do things to yourself

I never said give up control
I never said stick a needle in your arm and die
It wasn't me, it wasn't me, it wasn't me
I know he's dead but it wasn't me

It wasn't me who shamed you, who covered you with mud
You did it to yourself without any help from me
You act as if I could've told you or stopped you like some god
But people never listen and you know that that's a fact

I never said slit your wrists and die
I never said throw your life away
It wasn't me, it wasn't me, it wasn't me
You're killing yourself—you can't blame me

it wasn't me it wasn't me it wasn't me it wasn't me it wasn't me it wasn't me it wasn't me it wasn't me it wasn't me it wasn't me it wasn't me it wasn't me it wasn't me it wasn't me
it wasn't me it wasn't me it wasn't me it wasn't me it wasn't me it wasn't me it wasn't me it wasn't me it wasn't me it wasn't me it wasn't me it wasn't me it wasn't me it wasn't me
it wasn't me it wasn't me it wasn't me it wasn't me it wasn't me it wasn't me it wasn't me it wasn't me it wasn't me it wasn't me it wasn't me it wasn't me it wasn't me it wasn't me
it wasn't me it wasn't me it wasn't me it wasn't me it wasn't me it wasn't me it wasn't me it wasn't me it wasn't me it wasn't me it wasn't me it wasn't me it wasn't me it wasn't me

I Believe

Valerie Solanis took the elevator got off at the 4th floor
Valerie Solanis took the elevator got off at the 4th floor
She pointed the gun at Andy saying you
cannot control me anymore

I believe there's got to be some retribution
I believe an eye for an eye is elemental
I believe there's something wrong if she's alive right now

Valerie Solanis took three steps, pointing at the floor
Valerie Solanis waved her gun, pointing at the floor
From inside her idiot madness spoke and bang
Andy fell onto the floor

I believe life's serious enough for retribution
I believe being sick is no excuse and
I believe I would've pulled the switch on her myself

When they got him to the hospital his pulse was gone
They thought that he was dead
His guts were pouring from his wounds onto the floor
They thought that he was dead
Not until years later would the hospital do to him
What she could not
What she could not
"Where were you, you didn't come to see me"
Andy said, "I think I died, why didn't you come to see me"
Andy said, "It hurt so much, they took blood from my hand"

I believe there's got to be some retribution
I believe there's got to be some restitution
I believe we are all the poorer for it now

Visit me, visit me
Visit me, visit me
Visit me, why didn't you visit me
Visit me, why didn't you visit me

Andy Andy Andy Andy Andy Andy Andy Andy Andy Andy

Andy Andy Andy Andy Andy

you
you
you
you
you
you
you
you
you
you
you
you
you
you
you
you
you
you
you
you
you
you
you
you
you

Nobody But You

I really care a lot although I look like I do not
Since I was shot—there's nobody but you
I know I look blasé, "party Andy"'s what the papers say
At dinner I'm the one who pays—for a nobody like you
Nobody but you, a nobody like you
Since I got shot there's nobody but you

Won't you decorate my house
I'll sit there quiet as a mouse
You know me I like to look a lot—at nobody but you
I'll hold your hand and slap my face
I'll tickle you to your disgrace
Won't you put me in my proper place—a nobody like you

Sundays I pray a lot, I'd like to wind you up
And paint your clock
I want to be what I am not—for a nobody like you

The bullet split my spleen and lung, the doctors said I was gone
Inside I've got some shattered bone—for nobody but you
Nobody but you, nobody like you
Shattered bone for nobody but you

I'm still not sure I didn't die
And if I'm dreaming I still have bad pains inside
I know I'll never be a bride—to nobody like you
I wish I had a stronger chin, my skin was good, my nose was thin
This is no movie I'd ask to be in—with a nobody like you
Nobody like you, a nobody like you
All my life—it's been nobodies like you

A Dream

It was a very cold clear fall night. I had a terrible dream. Billy Name and Brigid were playing under my staircase on the second floor about two o'clock in the morning. I woke up because Amos and Archie had started barking. That made me very angry because I wasn't feeling well and I told them. I was very cross, the real me, that they just better remember what happened to Sam the Bad Cat that was left at home and got sick and went to pussy heaven.

It was a very cold clear fall night. Some snowflakes were falling. Gee it was so beautiful, and so I went to get my camera to take some pictures. And then I was taking the pictures but the exposure thing wasn't right and I was going to call Fred or Gerry to find out how to get it set but, oh, it was too late and then I remembered they were still probably at dinner and anyway I felt really bad and didn't want to talk to anybody. But the snowflakes were so beautiful and real looking and I really wanted to hold them. And that's when I heard the voices from down the hall near the stairs. So I got a flashlight and I was scared and I went out into the hallway. There's been all kinds of trouble lately in the neighborhood and someone's got to bring home the bacon and anyway there were Brigid and Billy playing. And under the staircase was a little meadow sort of like the park at 23rd street where all the young kids go and play frisbee. Gee that must be fun, maybe we should do an article on that in the magazine, but they'll just tell me I'm stupid and it won't sell. But I'll hold my ground this time, I mean it's my magazine isn't it?

So I was thinking that as the snowflakes fell and I heard these voices having so much fun. Gee it would be so great to have some fun. So I called Billy, but either he didn't hear me or he didn't want to answer, which was so strange because even if I don't like reunions I've always loved Billy. I'm so glad he's working. I mean it's different than Ondine. He keeps touring with those movies and he doesn't even pay us and the film, I mean the film's just going to disintegrate and then what. I mean he's so normal off of drugs. I just don't get it.

And then I saw John Cale. And he's been looking really great. He's been coming by the office to exercise with me. Ronnie said I have a muscle but he's been really mean since he went to AA. I mean what does it mean when you give up drinking and you're still so mean. He says I'm being lazy but I'm not, I just can't find any ideas. I mean I'm just not, let's face it, going to get any ideas up at the office.

And seeing John made me think of the Velvets and I had been thinking about them when I was on St. Marks Place going to that new gallery those sweet new kids have opened, but they thought I was old, and then I saw the old Dom, the old club where we did our first shows. It was so great. I don't understand about that Velvet's first album. I mean I did the cover and I was the producer and I always see it repackaged and I've never gotten a penny from it. How could that be. I should call Henry. But it was good seeing John, I did a cover for him, but I did in black and white and he changed it to color. It would have been worth more if he'd left it my way but you can never tell anybody anything, I've learned that.

ano ther ano ther ano ther ano ther

ano ther ano ther ano ther ano ther

I tried calling again to Billy and John but they wouldn't recognize me it was like I wasn't there. Why won't they let me in. And then I saw Lou. I'm so mad at him. Lou Reed got married and didn't invite me. I mean is it because he thought I'd bring too many people. I don't get it. He could have at least called. I mean he's doing so great. Why doesn't he call me? I saw him at the MTV show and he was one row away and he didn't even say hello. I don't get it. You know I hate Lou I really do. He won't even hire us for his videos. And I was so proud of him.

I was so scared today. There was blood leaking through my shirt from those old scars from being shot. And the corset I wear to keep my insides in was hurting. And I did three sets of 15 pushups and 4 sets of ten situps. But then my insides hurt and I saw drops of blood on my shirt and I remember the doctors saying I was dead. And then later they had to take blood out of my hand 'cause they'd run out of veins but then all this thinking was making me an old grouch and you can't do anything anyway so if they wouldn't let me play with them in my own dream. I was just going to have to make another and another and another. Gee wouldn't it just be so funny if I died in this dream before I could make another one up.

And nobody called.

ano ther ano ther ano ther ano ther

ano ther ano ther ano ther ano ther

Forever Changed

Train entering the city
I lost myself—and never came back
Took a trip 'round the world—and never came back
Black silhouettes, crisscrossed tracks—never came back

You might think I'm frivolous—uncaring and cold
You might think I'm empty—depends on your point of view
Society Andy who paints and records them
The high and the low—never turn back

Got to get to the city—get a job
Got to get some work—to see me through
My old life's behind—I see it receding
My life's disappearing—disappearing from view

Hong Kong and I was changed
Burma Thailand—and I was changed
A few good friends—to see me through
Henry and Brigid—to see me through
Only art—to see me through
Only heart—to see me through
My old life's disappearing—disappearing from view

Forever changed, forever changed
I was forever changed

Hello It's Me

Andy it's me, haven't seen you in a while
I wish I'd talked to you more when you were alive
I thought you were self-assured when you acted shy
Hello it's me

I really miss you, I really miss your mind
I haven't heard ideas like that for such a long long time
I loved to watch you draw and watch you paint
But when I saw you last, I turned away

When Billy Name was sick and locked up in his room
You asked me for some speed, I thought it was for you
I'm sorry if I doubted your good heart
Things always seem to end before they start

Hello it's me, that was a great gallery show
Your cow wallpaper and your floating silver pillows
I wish I paid more attention when they laughed at you
Hello it's me

"Pop goes pop artist," the headline said
"Is shooting a put on, is Warhol really dead?"
You get less time for stealing a car
I remember thinking as I heard my own record in a bar

They really hated you, now all that's changed
But I have some resentments that can never be unmade
You hit me where it hurt I didn't laugh
Your Diaries are not a worthy epitaph

Oh well now Andy—I guess we've got to go
I wish someway somehow you like this little show
I know this is late in coming but it's the only way I know
Hello it's me—good night Andy
Goodbye Andy

good night

good night

good night

good night

good night

good night

good night

good night

good night

good night

good night

good night

good night

good night

good night

good night

good night

good night

good night

good night

357

good night

LOU REED
LOU REED
MAGIC AND LOSS
MAGIC AND LOSS

What's Good—The Thesis

Life's like a mayonnaise soda
And life's like space without room
And life's like bacon and ice cream
That's what life's like without you

Life's like forever becoming
But life's forever dealing in hurt
Now life's like death without living
That's what life's like without you

Life's like Sanskrit read to a pony
I see you in my mind's eye strangling on your tongue
What good is knowing such devotion
I've been around—I know what makes things run

What good is seeing-eye chocolate
What good's a computerized nose
And what good was cancer in April
Why no good—no good at all

What good's a war without killing
What good is rain that falls up
What good's a disease that won't hurt you
Why no good, I guess, no good at all

What good are these thoughts that I'm thinking
It must be better not to be thinking at all
A styrofoam lover with emotions of concrete
No not much, not much at all

What good is life without living
What good's this lion that barks
You loved a life others throw away nightly
It's not fair, not fair at all

What's good?
What's good?
Not much at all
Life's good —
But not fair at all

Power And Glory—The Situation

I was visited by the Power and the glory
I was visited by a majestic hymn
Great bolts of lightning
Lighting up the sky
Electricity flowing through my veins

I was captured by a larger moment
I was seized by divinity's hot breath
Gorged like a lion on experience
Powerful from life
I want all of it—
Not just some of it

I saw a man turn into a bird
I saw a bird turn into a tiger
I saw a man hang from a cliff by the tips of his toes
In the jungles of the Amazon
I saw a man put a redhot needle through his eye
Turn into a crow and fly through the trees
Swallow hot coals and breathe out flames
And I wanted this to happen to me

We saw the moon vanish into his pocket
We saw the stars disappear from sight
We saw him walk across the water into the sun
While bathed in eternal light
We spewed out questions waiting for answers
Creating legends, religions and myths
Books, stories, movies and plays
All trying to explain this

I saw a great man turn into a little child
The cancer reduce him to dust
His voice growing weak as he fought for his life
With a bravery few men know
I saw isotopes introduced into his lungs
Trying to stop the cancerous spread
And it made me think of Leda and the Swan
And gold being made from lead
The same power that burned Hiroshima
Causing three-legged babies and death
Shrunk to the size of a nickel
To help him regain his breath
And I was struck by the power and the glory
I was visited by a majestic Him
Great bolts of lightning lighting up the sky
As the radiation flowed through him
He wanted all of it
Not some of it

Magician—Internally

Magician magician take me upon your wings
And gently roll the clouds away
I'm sorry so sorry I have no incantations
Only words to help sweep me away
I wan t some magic to sweep me away
I want some magic to sweep me away
I want to count to five
T urn around and find myself g o n e
Fl y me throug h the stor m
A nd wake up in the ca l m

R eleas e me fr om thi s bo d y
Fr om this bulk t hat mo ves b es ide m e
L et me leave this bo dy far a wa y
I' m sick of looking at me
I hate this painful body
T hat disease has slowly worn away

Magician take my spirit
Inside I'm young and vital
Inside I'm alive—please take me away
So many things to do—it's too early
For my life to be ending
For this body to simply rot away

I want some magic to keep me alive
I want a miracle I don't want to die
I'm afraid that if I go to sleep I'll never wake
I'll no longer exist
I'll close my eyes and disappear
And float into the mist

Somebody please hear me
My hand can't hold a cup of coffee
My fingers are weak—things just fall away
Inside I'm young and pretty
Too many things unfinished
My very breath taken away

Doctor you're no magician—and I am no believer
I need more than faith can give me now
I want to believe in miracles—not just belief in numbers
I need some magic to take me away

I want some magic to sweep me away
I want some magic to sweep me away
Visit on this starlit night
Replace the stars the moon the light—the sun's gone
Fly me through this storm
And wake up in the calm ...
I fly right through this storm
And I wake up in the calm

Sword of Damocles—Externally

I see the Sword of Damocles is right above your head
They're trying a new treatment to get you out of bed
But radiation kills both bad and good
It can not differentiate
So to cure you they must kill you
The Sword of Damocles hangs above your head

Now I've seen lots of people die
From car crashes or drugs
Last night on 33rd Street I saw a kid get hit by a bus
But this drawn out torture over which part of you lives
Is very hard to take
To cure you they must kill you
The Sword of Damocles above your head

That mix of Morphine and Dexedrine
We use it on the street
It kills the pain and keeps you up
Your very soul to keep
But this guessing game has its own rules
The good don't always win
And might makes right
The Sword of Damocles
Is hanging above your head

It seems everything's done that must be done
From over here, though, things don't seem fair
But there are things that we can't know
Maybe there's something over there
Some other world that we don't know about
I know you hate that mystic shit
It's just another way of seeing
The Sword of Damocles above your head

Goodbye Mass—In a Chapel Bodily Termination

Sitting on a hard chair try to sit straight
Sitting on a hard chair this moment won't wait
Listening to the speakers—they're talking about you
Look at all the people, all the people you knew

Sitting with my back straight it becomes hard to hear
Some people are crying it becomes hard to hear
I don't think you'd have liked it you would have made a jo ke
You would have made it easier you'd say, "Tomor row I 'm s mo k e"

Sitting on a hard chair how far we have come
Trying hard to listen to your friends who have co me
Some of them are famous and some are j ust like me
Trying hard to listen trying hard to see

Sitting on a hard chair it's over . . . time to stand
Some people are crying I turn to grab yo u r hand
It's your daughter saying thank you
You, you would have made a joke
"Isn't this something," you'd say, "T o m o r r ow I' m s m
o k
e "

Cremation—Ashes to Ashes

Well the coalblack sea waits for me me me
The coalblack sea waits forever
The waves hit the shore
Crying more more more
But the coalblack sea waits forever

The tornadoes come, up the coast they run
Hurricanes rip the sky forever
Though the weathers change
The sea remains the same
The coalblack sea waits forever

There are ashes spilt through collective guilt
People rest at sea forever
Since they burnt you up
Collect you in a cup
For you the coalblack sea has no terror

Will your ashes float like some foreign boat
Or will they sink absorbed forever
Will the Atlantic coast
Have its final boast
Nothing else contained you ever

Now the coalblack sea waits for me me me
The coalblack sea waits forever
When I leave this joint
At some further point
The same coalblack sea will it be waiting

Dreamin'—Escape

If I close my eyes I see your face and I'm not without you
If I try hard and concentrate, I can still hear you speak
I picture myself in your room by the chair
You're smoking a cigarette
If I close my eyes I can see your face you're saying, "I missed you"
Dreamin'—I'm always dreamin'

If I close my eyes I can smell your perfume—you look and say, "Hi babe"
If I close my eyes pictures from China still hang from the wall
I hear the dog bark I turn and say, "What were you saying?"
I picture you in the red chair inside the pale room

You sat in your chair with a tube in your arm—you were so skinny
You were still making jokes (I don't know what drugs they had you on)
You said, "I guess this is not the time for long-term investments"
You were always laughing, but you never laughed at me

They say in the end the pain was so bad that you were screaming
Now you were no saint, but you deserved better than that
From the corner I watched them removing things from your apartment
But I can picture your red chair and pale room inside my head

If I close my eyes I see your face and I'm not without you
If I try hard and concentrate I can hear your voice saying,
"Who better than you"
If I close my eyes I can't believe that I'm here without you
Inside your pale room your empty red chair and my head
Dreamin'—I'm always dreamin'

No Chance—Regret

It must be nice to be steady, it must be nice to be f irm
It must be nice never to move off of the mark
It m ust be nice to be de p end able and ne ver l et any one down
It m u s t be great to be all the things you're not
It m u st be great to be all the things that I'm not

I se e yo u in the hospital y our hu mo r is intact
I'm e m bar rass ed by the st ren gth I se em to lac k
If I was in your shoes
So strange that I am not
I'd fo ld up in a minute and a half
I'd fo ld u p in a minute and a half
A n d I didn't get a chance to say goodbye

It m u st be nice to b e no rm al it must be nice to be cold
It m u st be nice no t t o h ave to go, oh, up or down
Bu t me I'm allem o ti on al n o matter how I try
You'r e gone and I'm still here a live
You're go ne and I am still aliv e
And I d i dn't get a ch ance to say goo db ye
No — I di dn't get a ch ance to say go od bye

Th ere a re thi ngs we say we wish we k new an d in fact we never do
But I wi sh I'd known that you were going to die
Th en I wouldn't feel so stupid, such a f oo th at I d idn't call
And I didn't get a chance to say goodbye
I didn't get a chance to say goodbye

No there's no logic to this—who's picked to stay or go
If you think too hard it only makes you mad
But your optimism made me think you really had it beat
So I didn't get a chance to say goodbye
I didn't get a chance to say goodbye

The Warrior King—Revenge

I wish I was the warrior king in every language that I speak
Lord over all th at I surve yand all that I see I kee p
Power omnipres e nt u ndiminished uncontrolled
With a massive vi ol e nt fu r yat the center of m ysoul

I wish I was a w ar ri o r k in
With a faceless ch ar g in g in sc rutable beni gn
Footsteps so hea v y t h at g p o w er a lw a ys at
My rage instilli ng fear t h e w or l d s h a k es m y c o m m and
Ye tcau tious firm bu t fair an d goo d
The perfect warrior king

I wish I installed angels in every subject's house
Agents of my goodness no one would be without
A steak on every plate a car for every house
And if you ever crossed me
I'd have your eyes put out

You don't exist without me, without me you don't exist
And if logic won't convince you—then there's always this
I'm bigger, smarter, stronger, tough
Yet sensitive and kind
And though I could crush you like a bug
It would never cross my mind

It wouldn't cross my mind to break your neck
Or rip out your vicious tongue
It wouldn't cross my mind to snap your leg like a twig
Or squash you like some slug
You are a violent messenger
And I'm not above your taunts
And if you hit me you know I'll kill you
Because I'm the warrior king

Harry's Circumcision—Reverie Gone Astray

Looking in the mirror Harry didn't like what he saw
The cheeks of his mother, the eyes of his father
As each day crashed around him the future stood revealed
He was turning into his parents
The final disappointment

Stepping out of the shower, Harry stared at himself
His hairline receding, the slight overbite
He picked up the razor to begin his shaving
And thought—oh I wish I was different
I wish I was stronger I wish I was thinner
I wish I didn't have this nose
These ears that stick out remind me of my father
And I don't want to be reminded at all
The final disappointment

Harry looked in the mirror thinking of Vincent van Gogh
And with a quick swipe lopped off his nose
And happy with that he made a slice where his chin was
He'd always wanted a dimple
The end of all illusion
Then peering down straight between his legs
Harry thought of the range of possibilities
A new face a new life no m emories of the past
A n d slit his throat fr om e a r to ear

H arry woke u p wi th a c ou g h—the stitches made him wince
A doctor s m i l ed at h im fr o m somewhere across the room
Son we s a v e d y ou r l ife bu t you'll never look the same
And w h e n h e h ear d th a t, H arry had to laugh
And w h e n h e h ear d th a t! H arry had to laugh
An d w h e n it h u r t H ar ry ha d to laugh
A l th ou g h
T h e fi n a l d is a p poi nt m e nt

Gassed and Stoked—Loss

Well, you covered your tracks
And now I can't see you
You had your ashes scattered at sea
There's no grave to visit, no tombstone to look at
You were in the New York Times obituary
There's no record no tape no book no movie
Some photographs and memories
Sometimes I dial your phone number by mistake
And this is what I hear
"This is no longer a working number baby
Please redial your call
This is no longer a working number
Your party doesn't live here anymore
This is no longer a working number
If you still require help
Stay on the line and an operator
W i l l try to bail you out"

I k new I should have seen you that Thursday
I k ne w I should n ' t have left
so good, your spirits so up
d ed
But yo u soun
y ou next week
ee
I thoug h t I'd s er if I had half a brain
ov
nd
I say over a a in in my head
br
f a
dialing a wrong number
re
If I had ha l
it h e
hat some recording said
w
I w ouldn't s to
ng
i
A n d lis ten

I knew I should have written, written things down
I always say I'll never forget
Who can forget a one-eyed pilot
Who's a concert pianist
A painter a poet songwriter supreme
My friends are blending in my head
They're melding into one Great Spirit
And that spirit isn't dead

Now I may not remember everything that you said
But I remember all the things you've done
And not a day goes by not an hour
When I don't try to be like you
You were gassed, stoked and rarin' to go
And you were that way all of the time
So I guess you know why I'm laughing at myselves
Every time I dial the wrong line
This is no longer a working number, baby
Gassed stoked and ready to go
Gassed stoked and ready to go
Gassed stoked and ready to go

Power and The Glory. Part II—Magic • Transformation

With a bravery stronger than lust
— Shooting up his veins

Magic and Loss—The Summation

When you pass through the fire
You pass through humble
You pass through a maze of self-doubt
When you pass through humble
The lights can blind you
Some people never figure that out
You pass through arrogance you pass through hurt
You pass through an ever-present past
And it's best not to wait for luck to save you
Pass through the fire to the light

As you pass through the fire
Your right hand waving
There are things you have to throw out
That caustic dread inside your head
Will never help you out
You have to be very strong
'Cause you'll start from zero
Over and over again
And as the smoke clears
There's an all-consuming fire
Lying straight ahead

They say no one person can do it all
But you want to in your head
But you can't be Shakespeare
And you can't be Joyce
So what is left instead
You're stuck with yourself

And a rage that can hurt you
You have to start at the beginning again
And just this moment
This wonderful fire started up again

When you pass through humble
When you pass through sickly
When you pass through
I'm better than you all
When you pass through
Anger and self-deprecation
And have the strength to acknowledge it all
When the past makes you laugh
And you can savor the magic
That let you survive your own war
You find that that fire is passion
And there's a door up ahead not a wall

As you pass through fire as you pass through fire
Try to remember its name
When you pass through fire licking at your lips
You cannot remain the same
And if the buildi ng's burning
Move towards t hat door
But don't put the fla mes o ut
There's a bit of mag ic in e veryth i n g
And then some l oss to ev e n thin gs o ut

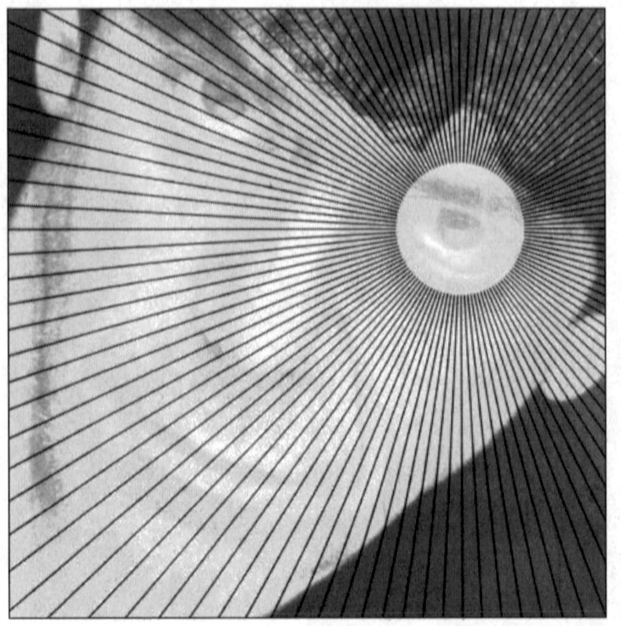

Egg Cream

When I was a young man—no bigger than this
A chocolate Egg Cream was not to be missed
Some U Bet's Chocolate Syrup, seltzer water mixed with milk
Stir it up into a heady fro—tasted just like silk

Now you can go to Junior's, Dave's on Canal Street
I think there's Kens in Boston
There must be something in L.A.
But Becky's on Kings Highway
Was the Egg Cream of choice
If you don't believe me
Go ask any of the boys

The only good thing I remember about P.S. 92
Was the Egg Cream served at Becky's
It was a fearsome brew
For 50 cents you got a shot—chocolate bubbles up your nose
Made it easier to deal with knife fights and kids pissing in the street

So the next time you're in Brooklyn—please say hello for me
Totonno's for pizza and ice cream at Al and Shirley's
But mostly you go to Becky's—sit in a booth and say hello
And have two chocolate Egg Creams—one to stay and go

You scream, I steam, we all want Egg Cream

NYC Man

It can only lead to trouble if you break my heart
If you accidentally crush it on the Ides of March
I'd prefer you were straightforward
You don't have to go through all of that
I'm a New York City man, baby
Say "Go" and that is that

It's far too complicated to make up a lie
That you'd have to remember and really why
I wouldn't want to be around you
If you didn't want to have me around
I'm a m-a-n-n man
Blink your eyes and I'll be gone

Brutus made a pretty speech but Caesar was betrayed
Lady Macbeth went crazy but Macbeth ended slain
Ophelia and Desdemona dead leaving Hamlet in a play
But I'm no Lear with a blinded eye
Say "Go" and I am gone

The stars have shut their eyes up tight
The earth has changed its course
A kingdom sits on a black knight's back
As he tries to mount a white jeweled horse
While a clock full of butterflies on the hour
Releases a thousand moths
You say "Leave" and I'll be gone
Without any remorse
No letters, faxes, phones or tears
There's a difference between
Bad and worse

New York City I love you
Blink your eyes and I'll be gone
Just a little grain of sand

Finish Line (For Sterl)

Wind blows snow outside my window
Crowd below runs wild in the streets
Two rented brothers race down two separate alleys
Heading for the finish line

Down in the train yard out by the stockyard
Butchers with aprons hack meat in the snow
Blood has the brothers pulsing with envy
Heading for the finish line

Two rented brothers—their faces keep changing
Like these feelings I have for you
Nothing's forever not even five minutes
When you're headed for the finish line

Down by the depot out by the meat rack
Down by the tunnels surrounding the jails
Prisoners are marching in squares and in circles
They're heading for the finish line

They're lining up for Noah's Ark
They're stabbing each other in the dark
Saluting a flag made of some rich guy's socks
Heading for the finish line

Close to the line the ice is cracking
Two rented feelings sitting in the stands
Two mothers, two fathers and both of them are paid for
All of a sudden it comes back to me

Just up ahead is the finish line
Two rented referees and two checkered rags
Out of the corner of my eye comes a
Dark horse with black wings
Headed for the finish line

I'm five years old the room is fuzzy
I think there's also a very young girl
It's so hard to remember what happened exactly
As I'm staring at the finish line

First came fire then came light
Then came feeling then came sight

Trade In

I met a new me at 8 A.M.
The other one got lost
This was not a trade in
Although I wouldn't believe the cost
I woke up crying as we said goodbye
Me and my old self
Each day he vanished more and more
As I became someone else

He actually was murdered
I had taken him apart
But when I put him back together
I couldn't find his heart
It was resting underneath a chair
In a bed of bright tinfoil
If I pulled back the flaps
I could still see it beat
I could still hear his voice uncoil
As I said:

I want a trade in
A 14th chance at this life
I met a woman with a thousand faces
And I want to make her my wife

How could I have been so mistaken
How could I think that it was true
A child that is raised by an idiot
And that idiot then becomes you

How could I believe in a movie
How could I believe in a book
But most of all how could I listen to you
Such an obvious schmuck
A life spent listening to assholes
It's funny but it's true
So get rid of them I said to myself
But first I'm—I'm getting rid of you

Take me over to the window
My heart said to my head
Please set me on fire
So we can start again
I was so wrong that it's funny
And I can't apologize
But instead,
You can be everything that I'm not
The second that I die

Hang On to Your Emotions

When your imagination has too much to say
When the chill of the night meets the sweat of the day
And you have trouble understanding what other people have to say
You'd better hang on to your emotions

When a demagogue inside your head has taken charge
And by default what you say or do is criticized
And this litany of failures is recited a thousand times
You'd better hang on to your emotions

Could it be you've never felt like that
That your mind's a cage inside the cage a cat
That spits and scratches all it can get at
And that's you
And your emotions

Could it be you've never felt like that
Your mind's a cage inside the cage a rat
Rabidly trying to get at
You and your emotions
You and your emotions

When your imagination has too much to say
When that facile voice inside your head says give your life away
You might think to ask how it got that way
What books it has read that make it that way
And where it got the right to speak to anyone that way
You'd better hold on to your emotions
Hold on to your emotions

When a night city's breeze blows across the room
And a 5 A.M. moon and sun start their swoon
You hear your lover's breath
And not a moment too soon
You get to release all your emotions
You get to let go of your emotions

I want to let go
I want to release now

Sex with Your Parents (Motherfucker) Part II

I was thinking of things that I hate to do
Things you do to me or I do to you
Something fatter and uglier than Rush Rambo
Something more disgusting than Robert Dole
Something pink that climbs out of a hole
And there it was—sex with your parents

I was getting so sick of this rightwing Republican shit
These ugly old men scared of young tit and dick
So I tried to think of something that made me sick
And there it was—sex with your parents

Now these old fucks can steal all they want
And they can go and pass laws saying you can't say what you want
And you can't look at this and you can't look at that
And you can't smoke this and you can't snort that
And me, baby—I got statistics—I got stats
These people have been to bed with their parents

Now I know you're shocked but hang and have a brew
If you think about it for a minute you know that it's true
They're ashamed and repelled
They don't know what to do
They've had sex with their parents
When they looked into their lovers' eyes they saw mom

In the name of family values we must ask whose family
In the name of family values we must ask:

Senator, it's been reported that you have had
Illegal congress with your mother
Senator an illegal congress by proxy is a
Pigeon by any other name

Senators you polish a turd
Here in the big city we got a word
For those who would bed their beloved big bird
And make a mockery of our freedoms
Without even using a condom
Without even saying "No"
By God we have a name for people like that
It's—hey Motherfucker

Hookywooky

I'm standing with you on your roof
Looking at the chemical sky
All purple blue and oranges,
Some pigeons flying by
The traffic on Canal Street is so noisy—it's a shock
And someone's shooting fireworks
Or a gun on the next block
Traffic's so noisy it's a shock
Sounds like fireworks
Or a gun on the next block
I want to hookywooky with you

Your ex-lover Satchel is here from France
Yet another ex!
They gather about you like a Mother Superior
All of you still friends
But none of my old flames ever talk to me
When things end for me they end
They take your pants your money your name
But the song still remain

You're so civilized it hurts
I guess I could learn a lot
About people, plants and relationships
How not to get hurt a lot
And each lover I meet up on your roof
I wouldn't want to throw him off

Mmm, into the chemical sky
Down into the streets to die
Under the wheels of a car on Canal Street
And each lover I meet up on your roof
I wouldn't want to throw him off
Into the chemical sky
Under the wheels of a car to die on Canal Street

The Proposition

You can't have the flower without the root
You can't have the fire without the soot
Even a stripper needs her red tasseled suit
And we were meant to be

In every war the north needs the south
And everyone knows all assholes have a mouth
Without mystery what would writers talk about
We were meant to be

An apple needs pits the way a melon needs seeds
Your foot needs your arm and your arm needs your knee
And one of these days I know you will need me
We were meant to be

Your mother's an ogre, your father's a scamp
You won't see my parents honored on any stamp
But just like a bulb screws into a lamp
We were meant to be

The way AIDS needs a vaccine
Somewhere a vaccine needs AIDS
The way a victim needs life
A life needs to be saved
And out of all of this
Will come a better way
We were meant to be

So you can go to Europe, Los Angeles or Mars
You can stand on a building
Throwing cinderblocks at cars
You can practice deep voodoo
But like me you'll see
We were meant to be

The Adventurer

You're an adventurer
You sail across the oceans
You climb the Himalayas
Seeking truth and beauty as a natural state
You're a queen reborn
Worshipped from above afar
Some see you as an elixir
An elemental natural seeking perfect grace
In a catacomb
Or cave of endless drawings
Prehistoric or religious
Your accomplishments prodigious
Seeking out the perfect tone
Your language so clear
Your voice perfectly turning
As in the city I sit yearning
Blowing rings of smoke from thin cigars
Or driving fast in foreign cars
To capture your remains

You're an adventurer
A turban wet wrapped 'round your head
On the mountainside they predict your death
Oh how you fooled them all
But subjects are a poor excuse
When what you really want's a muse
An inspirating knowledge of what comes before

Speeds of light
The momentary flicker of a candle
In its wicker basket
Smoking wax—Facts!
Did you find that superior knowledge
That eluded you in college
Did you find that super vortex
That could cause your cerebral cortex
To lose its grip
You're an adventurer
You were out looking for meaning
While the rest of us were steaming
In an inspirating urban pit
An adventurer
You enter as I'm dreaming
I wish I'd never wake up
Differentiating scheming from my one true love

You're an adventurer
You love the angles and the cherries
The height and width of levies
The natural bridge and tunnels of the human race
You're an adventurer
Nothing seems to scare you
And if it does it won't dissuade you
You just won't think about it
You dismiss it and defocus
You redefine the locus of your time in space—Race!
As you move further from me

And though I understand the thinking
And have often done the same thing I find parts of me gone
You're an adventurer
And though I'll surely miss you
And of course I'll survive without you
And maybe good will come of that
But at this point I anticipate some grieving
And although I know your leaving
Is a necessary adjunct to what we both do
An adventurer
Splitting up the atom
Splitting up the once was
Splitting up the essence
Of our star-crossed fate
None who meet you do forget you
My adventure
My adventure
My adventuress

Riptide

She's out of her mind
Like the wind in a storm
Like the ocean at dawn as it disappears, with the riptide

She's out of her mind
She's pulled away by the moon
She's ripped from her sleep as the cold lunar sweep gains control

What you gonna do with your emotions
Ones you barely recognize
In your sleep I heard you screaming
"This is not voluntary!
This is not voluntary!
If this is life I'd rather die!"
In the riptide

She's out of her mind—riptide
Like a muscle that swells
You know when you trip
Whether you're well or sick
Your body aches

She's out with the tide
Gone to a prisoner's dance
Where a monkey's her date
Eating limbs off a plate with a spoon

What you gonna do with your emotions

Said the seagull to the loon
What you gonna do with your emotions
She said, "Please wake me up."
She said, "Don't touch me now."
She said, "I wish I was dead."
With the riptide

She's out of her mind—riptide—you always win
It happens over and over again, riptide
She's out of her mind like a hurricane's rain
She does not stand a chance at this lunar dance riptide

I was thinking of van Gogh's last painting
The wheatfields and the crows
Is that perhaps what you've been feeling
When you see the ground
As you fall from the sky
As the floor disappears
From beneath your feet riptide

She's going out of her mind
Out with the tide
Out of her mind
With the riptide

Set the Twilight Reeling

Take me for what I am
A star newly emerging
Long-simmering explodes
Inside the self is reeling
In the pocket of the heart
In the rushing of the blood
In the muscle of my sex
In the mindful mindless love
I accept the new-found man and I set the twilight reeling

At 5 A.M. the moon and sun
Sit set before my window
Light glances off the blue glass we set
Right before the window
And you who accept
In your soul and your head
What was misunderstood
What was thought of with dread
A new self is borne
The other self dead
I accept the new-found man and set the twilight reeling

A soul singer stands on the stage
The spotlight shows him sweating
He sinks to one knee
Seems to cry
The horns are unrelenting
But as the drums beat he finds himself growing hard
In the microphone's face he sees her face growing large
And the swelling crescendo no longer retards
I accept the new-found man and set the twilight reeling

As the twilight sunburst gleams
As the chromium moon it sets
As I lose all my regrets and set the twilight reeling
I accept the new-found man and set the twilight reeling

Ocean - Here comes the ocean and the waves down by the sea / Here comes the ocean and the waves where have they been / Silver and black lit night / Here's to a summer's night / An empty splendid castle // Glowering alone at night / The princess has had a fight / Madness seeks out a lover // And here come the waves down by the shore / Washing the soul / Of the body that comes / From the depth of the sea / Here comes the ocean and the waves down by the sea / Here comes the ocean and the waves where have they been / Don't swim tonight my love / The tide is out my love / Malcolms curse haunts our family / Odious loud and rich / Ruler of filthy seas / Revel in heaven's justice // Here comes the waves and save for a scream / There's much like a song to be heard in the wind / That blows by the sea / By the wind down by the sea / Here come the waves

You Can Dance - Yeah, you can dance / With your only one / Yeah, you can dance / And have your fuckin' fun / Yeah, you can cry / With your only one / But I'll tell you / Hey honey that I won't be back again // Yeah, you can laugh HAH / 'Til you start to cry / You can dance, dance / Until you cry / Yeah, you can dance / Yeah, you can dance / Yeah yeah dance dance dance dance dance / Yeah, you can dance / Yeah, you can dance / Ah pull your ass baby and dance // Yeah, you can laugh / 'Til you start to fall / You can carry on / But I don't think that you're still tall / You can go around and carry on / With your only one / But I tell you something else honey / I'm not coming back no more / You can act like your gonna cry / You can laugh 'til your fuckin' heart strikes / You can laugh / Yeah, you can dance / Yeah, you can dance dance dance dance dance / You can dance / Yeah, you can dance / Stay here, I tell you to dance // You can laugh HAH / 'Til you start to cry and / You can carry on 'til your way dry / And you can dance / 'Til your life is gone but me / I'm not coming back again // Yeah, you can dance and dance and dance / Until your heart runs dry / You can carry on until I hope that you die / And you can dance / Yeah you can dance / Yeah, you can dance dance dance dance dance / Yeah, you can dance / Yeah, you can dance / Hey move your ass and dance

Such a Pretty Face - such a pretty face / and it was such a waste / and such a pretty face / it was such a disgrace / and such a pretty face / and it was such a waste / it was such a waste / such a pretty face / and it was such a waste

Affirmative Action (PO #99) - Hey patrolman number 44 / I'd like to see ya on the floor / Hey patrolman number 99 / I like to make it with you sometime // There's nothing the lawless would rather see / Than a patrolman down upon his knees sayin' / Please / Street hassle // There's nothing the lawless would rather see / Than a patrolman down upon his knees / I think the lawless she's very hot / She goes uptown then gets a hormone shot / There's nothing she would rather, rather see / Than a patrolman down on his knees // Hey patrolman number 99 / Hey officer I'd like to have you sometime / And patrolman number 44 / I'd like you to go down on me some more / There's nothing the lawless would rather see / Than a patrolman down on his knees sayin' / Please / Street hassle // Bang bang baby in the street / A policeman laying by my feet / What was the thing that you said last night / That made me wanna go start a fight / When I saw the body in the street / It made me feel like I would get weaker / There's nothing the lawless would rather see / Than a patrolman on his knees // Hey patrolman number 44 / I'd like to really get to see you some more / Hey patrolman number 99 / I'd like to get together with you sometime // We were looking for a street hassle

Better Get Up and Dance - Dance dance gotta get up and dance / Better dance dance dance gotta get up and dance / Get outta the bed man if you're low / Better get up and dance / Don't just sit around waiting for the phone / Better get up and dance / Better dance dance gotta get up and dance / Better dance dance dance gotta get up and dance // Baby don't you know you're wasting such time / Better get up and dance / Don't you say it all can't be mine / Better get up and dance / Better dance dance better get up and dance / Better dance dance dance better get up and dance / Better dance dance better get up and dance / Better dance dance dance better get up and dance // Baby you're nothing when you're all alone / Better get up and dance / Don't you sit and wait by the phone / Better get up and dance / Better dance dance better get up and dance / Better dance dance dance better get up and dance

Here Comes the Bride - I just wanna tell you a story / It happened to a friend of mine / Didn't have no power and no glory / Said he didn't have the time / He said he was a happy kind of person / Do anything to find out about this girl / She went and then she married another fella / Knocked my friend right out of this world / He heard the preacher say / Here comes the bride . . . / And doesn't she look lovely // Somebody call his Aunt Carrie / And tell her that her nephew Jimmy / Is comin' in from Vermont via the coast / And somebody call up his old man / Tell him that his son's arriving / And he's looking like a ghost // And somebody find that Virgin Mary / Oh won't you tell that bitch / Your Jimmy's a comin' back home / And somebody tell those ladies in waiting / HOLD IT NOW!! / Don't tell the preacher go on with it / We don't wanna hear those words / Here comes the bride / And doesn't she look lovely

My Name Is Mok - My name is Mok, thanks a lot / I know you love the thing I got / You've never seen the likes of me / Why I'm the biggest thing since WWIII // My name is Mok and I'm on fire / I'm the match and I'm the pyre / I'm the voodoo black musician priest / Why I'm the greatest thing since WWIII // My name is Mok, thanks a lot / I'm the power Sodom used on Lot / I am the pillar, I am the snake / I'm the beat that makes you shake / Why I'm the top, the point, the end / I'm more than a lover and more than a friend / I am the power of pure desire / My magic will take you higher / Than you've ever been before / So follow me beyond the door / Of the stupid hopes and dreams you've got // My name is Mok, thanks a lot / Girls . . . . // His name is Mok, thanks a lot / You think he's acting but he's not / The show that you're about to see / Is the absolutely finest greatest / Wonderment since WWIII // My name is Mok, thanks a lot / Just wait'll you see what I have got / There is nothing up my sleeve / Come look at this / There's nothing compared to me / I am the killer, I am the source / And you will worship me of course / I'm the oracle, I'm the seer, the wit / There is no question that I am it / I know what you've been waiting for / You won't have to wait no more / History reveals my friend, it reveals one thing / There's only one beginning and one end / There's only one, one and only is there not / My name is Mok, thanks a lot / Hey girls. . . . .

Little Sister - You know it's hard for me / I cannot use the phone / And in the shade of publicity no relationship is born / And I feel like a Hercules who's recently been shorn / but I have always loved my baby sister // Pick me up at eight / you'll see me on TV / I know I don't look well, time's not been good to me / But please believe me / the blame is all on me / and I've always loved my baby sister // Remember when / we were younger when / you would wait for me at school / and teachers, friends and brazen sins / and I was often cruel / But you always believed in me / you thought I was the best / And now that I've got you alone let me get this off my chest // Pick a melody then count from one to ten / I'll make a rhyme up and then we'll try again / to laugh or cry, or give a sigh / to a past that might have been / and how much I really loved my baby sister

Something Happened - Something happened I just don't understand / Something happened it's making me feel mad / Something happened you don't hear about / At least I never did before // Something happened I just don't understand / Something happened I just don't understand / Something happened it's making me feel mad / I never saw this on TV / I never read it in no book / Something happened I just don't understand // Something happened I just don't understand / Something happened it's making me feel mad / I thought I knew a lot of things / But I don't know a thing at all / Something happened I just don't understand / The things I hear and see / Don't seem the same / The things I touch and feel are forever changed / I've never felt this way before / And I hope I never do again / Something happened, I don't know why or when / Something happened, I just don't understand

Letters to the Vatican - Rosie sits inside a bar smoking a large man's cigar / In a place called "Sammy's" on Amsterdam Avenue / She doesn't look a day over 65, although she's really 29 / She likes records from the '60s / They remind her of the good old times // And after some wine and some scotch / Rosie starts to let it hang out: / She throws a glass at the mirror and asks Big Max for a pen // She writes a letter to the Vatican / "I'm gonna write a letter to Him: / Dear Pope, send me some soap and a bottle of Bombay gin" / A letter to the Vatican / "I'm gonna write a letter to Him: / Dear Pope, send me some hope or a rope to do me in" / And no one stops her / We all lend a hand / We all knew her before she was this mad / We just hold her until the shaking stops / Because the heart says what only the heart knows // "I wanna hear some Diana Ross / I wanna hear a little bit of Marvin Gaye / I wanna hear a song that reminds me of a better day" // Rosie slaps a pretty girl in the mouth / And running to the jukebox she tries to put a quarter in / She says, "I've had enough of you men / And I'll never say yes again; it's holiness or nothing / For me in this life . . . " // She writes a letter to the Vatican / "I'm gonna write a letter to him: / Dear Pope, send me some soap and a bottle of Bombay gin" / A letter to the Vatican / "I'm gonna write a letter to him: / Dear Pope, send me some hope or a rope to do me in // And no one stops her / We all lend a hand / We all knew her before she was this mad / We just hold her until the shaking stops / Because the heart says what only the heart knows

The Calm Before the Storm **-** There was a time when ignorance made our innocence strong / There was a time when we all thought we could do no wrong / There was a time, so long ago / but here we are in the calm before the storm // While the orchestra plays / they build barricades to help close the doors / While the musician sings / the holocaust rings the cymbals of war / We stare / at the things that were there / and no longer are— / And in our hearts / here we are again / In the calm before the storm // There was a time when we had an idea whose time hadn't come / They kept changing its name so we could still pretend / it was not really gone / We heard our screams turn into songs and back into screams again / And here we are again, / In the calm before the storm

One World One Voice **-** One World One Voice / Speakin' in a common tongue / Speakin' with a common drum / The drumming of your heart // One World One Voice / Speaking with a common tongue / Music speaks to everyone / And everyone speaks to it // One World One Voice / Each of us has our own choice / The choice whether to live or die / The music makes you smile // One World One Voice / Our commonness gives us a choice / And since we all are one / It's all or nothing at all // One World One Voice / Speaking in a common tongue / Speaking through guitars and drums / Making us all one // One World One Voice / Our commonness gives us a choice / And since we really all are one / It's all or nothing at all

Why Can't I Be Good **-** Why can't I be good, why can't I act like a man / Why can't I be good and do what other men can / Why can't I be good make something of this life / If I can't be a god let me be more than a wife / Why can't I be good // I don't want to be weak, I want to be strong / Not a fat happy weakling with two useless arms / A mouth that keeps moving with nothing to say / An eternal baby who never moved away // I'd like to look in a mirror with a feeling of pride / Instead of seeing a reflection of failure—a crime / I don't want to turn away to make sure I can not see / I don't want to hold my ears when I think about me // I want to be like the wind when it uproots a tree / Carries it across an ocean to plant in a valley / I want to be like the sun that makes it flourish and grow / I don't want to be what I am anymore // I was thinking of some kind of whacked-out syncopation / That would help improve this song / Some knock-'em down rhythm that would help move it along / Some rhyme of pure perfection,—a beat so hard and strong / If I can't get it right this time / Will a next time come along // Why can't I be good

You'll Know You Were Loved **-** Some things come to he who waits / But all is lost if you hesitate / And I was never one to wait / You'll know you were loved // You can hire great lawyers / You can speak to your friends / You can say we did this and that / Some things don't change // Unwrap the present and burn the remains / You'll know you were loved // Now you take Roscoe he ain't much / People say things are ruined after his touch / It's like a tar was dripping from his brush / But you'll know you were loved // Or Stan or Jake emerging from your past / From those love affairs that didn't last / But me I'll give it my last gasp / You'll know you were loved // A parrot a donkey a dog a bone / Some of us never had a home / And if we did we left it long ago / And didn't know we were loved // Empty as a wooden clock / Left in the woods at 12 o'clock / Insides all rusted, the spring has popped / But you'll know you were loved // Even when you sleep at night / Inside your heart will cry / You can never say goodbye / When you know you were loved // Underachievers of the world unite / You have nothing to lose except your fright / And together we can perhaps pass a night / When you know you were loved // And together we can perhaps / Pass a night when you know you were loved

Is Anybody Listening **-** Is anybody listening, is anybody out there / Is there anyone who listens to a poor man's song / Is it true our hearts are empty / That we are beyond caring / The sound of one hand clapping / Is a poor man's song // Is anybody listening to the story of oppression / Is everybody tired of the man who misses opportunity / Is everybody bored with one more story of debasement / Of the lone man once more humbled / Left beaten left for dead // Is everybody bored with stories of failure / Is everybody tired of the man who can't succeed / (Give me your hand) / Is the city finally empty of any pretense, sense of caring / Is it true that you are tired of a / Poor man on his knees // Is anybody listening, is anybody out there / Is anybody listening to this poor man's song / Howling in the rubble in the bowels within the city / Screaming for a fair chance / Smoke burning in his lungs // Is anybody listening, is anybody out there / If we all joined together making one united voice / The earth could move / The sky would shake / If we all sang together / The story of all poor men / Hear the city's cry // Is anybody listening to the soul of the big city / To the Appalachian Mountains, to the worker on his feet / Is anybody listening to the soul of West Virginia / To the farmer in the heartland / A convict putting in hard time // Is anybody listening, is somebody out there / Is anybody listening to a poor man's song / Is anybody out there for the man who's always working / And is thrown away like a paper plate / When a younger man comes along // Is anybody out there, is anybody listening / Is anybody listening to this poor man's song / Is anybody out there, can anybody hear me / The sound of one hand clapping is a poor man's song

Downtown Dirt (Prototype) - Pickin' up pieces of information / Down on the docks / Pickin' up pieces of information about you / And how to pick locks / Scoutin' around on the Lower East Side / A mattress is in the rain / Those uptown ladies with their uptown coats / Come down here to get laid // It's a boring macho trip / And I'm the type that fascinates // Hey, Mrs. Pamela Brown / How's the Dakota / You're twenty eight years old and your face has been lifted / But you still look so much older / Your bed is soiled your linen is drab / You got crabs / The things they sell you-your credit cards / I love you for 'em / I love you for it // I sell you sugar—I'm a humanitarian / I give it all to myself that way you're clean / And I stay out of debt // And psychologically, you know hey psychologically / It's better that I think I'm dirt / Psychologically it's better that I think that I'm dirt / Don't you know it's better that I think that I'm dirt // Hey don't you like to have some dirt / That's all it's worth its just dirt / Cheap / Cheap damn dirt // Hey Pam dirt / Cheap dirt / Worth dirt / Uptown dirt / Dirt

TIME ROCKER

Alone at Last

Alone at last
Hello I must be going
I met my self a year from today—what a shock!

Alone at last
Hello I must be coming
I ran into my self two years ago today—what a shock!

What did that girl look like
That I never married
I fly into the future and see her with a baby carriage
You didn't miss much old sport
You'd be in a pauper's court

Look into the future
Look into the past
Here I am alone at last
With history gone and tomorrows to come
I witnessed the invention of the atomic bomb
I saw my own death
Should I try to prevent it
And if I did—could I live forever
And never age and always be healthy
Could I change the times and become very wealthy
Would history change because I had viewed it
Alone at last
Alone at last
Alone at last

Here I am alone at last
A head on my shoulders
Legs under my ass
Before me the future
Behind me the past
The present always shifting

If I knew what I could do
One is one and two is two
But this is time I'll travel through
Alone at last
Alone at last
Future past

Blood of the Lamb

Who do you think you're kidding
The blood of the lamb is unforgiving
I'd rather have the head of the King of Siam
Or the heart of a prince from Pakistan

Who do you think you're kidding
This sacrifice is unforgiven
Next thing kill me a firstborn son
Bring me the cock of a tortured bull
The hand, the foot, the tongue, the brain of a m[illegible]

Who do you think you're kidding
The blood of the lamb is unforgiving
Bring me the ears of a pharaoh's wife
Barbaric love masquerades as hate

Who do you think you're kidding
The blood of the lamb is unforgiving
Blood on the altar blood on the feet
Blood on the landscape, oh what a creep
A river of blood is like a river of piss to me

Who do you think you're kidding
The blood of the lamb is unforgiving
The tooth of a king the scalp of a queen
The light of the stars the start of a scream

Who do you think you're kidding
The blood of the lamb can't be forgiven
Blood on the hands blood on the feet
Blood in the alleys blood in the street
Blood that won't wash off
A river of piss to me

Who do you think you're kidding
Who do you think you're kidding

Vanishing Act

It must be nice to disappear
To have a vanishing act
To always be moving forward and
Never looking back

How nice it is to disappear and
Float into a mist
With a young lady on your arm
Looking for a kiss

It might be nice to disappear
To have a vanishing act
To always be looking forward
Never look over your back

It must be nice to disappear
Float into a mist
With a young lady on your arm
Looking for a kiss

Float into the mist
Float into the mist
Disappear into the mist
And float into the mist

ongo and Longo

ongo: When Daddy died he made me a slave
ongo: Yes when Daddy died he left me everything
The tent the circus the cook this chair
Everything you see and smell including the air
ongo: And I, Mr. Mongo, get to forever serve you
ongo: And I, Mr. Longo, am glad that you do!

oth: Things have always been this way
One's the master one's the slave

ongo: Mr. Mongo bring me bread
The wine of insects with
An eight-year head
Some cockroach 30 with a fragrant musk
And serve it in Daddy's head by the bust

oth: How nice it is to be this way
ongo: He's the master
ongo: He's the slave
oth: Things have always been this way
One is master one is slave

ongo: I was left nothing so I have to behave
The fact is I'm happier being a slave
For I always do good and I don't have to think
I'm happier that way I think
There's too much stress and responsibility
Being the one who is always free
If I had a choice I would still remain me
Some are meant to serve

Longo: Let's drink a toast with
  Some old dead bug wine

Both: It's been that way since the beginning of time
Longo: I am the master he's the slave
Both: Things have always been this way

Longo: I was made for power
  It seems obvious now
  As beloved dead pater
  Was aware all along
  Some are born to greatness
  Some are born to crawl
  You know that it's true
  He can't make his mind up at all
  There's no question in my mind
  That it's better this way

Both: Things have always been this way
  One is master one is slave
  One is meant to serve

A Witness to Life

Historically helpless I stand without entering
I watch at a distance
My heart fairly melting—away
Consumed yet removed
I'm forever a witness
A taster not a drinker
Forever
A witness to life

Historically passive I stand always waiting
Forever observing
My heart palpitating
Awaiting a missive or some sort of signal
A kiss or a slap causing some sort of tingle in me

A witness to life

Gossip Song

Have you heard that she's pregnant? (NO!)
Yes she's pregnant again
My God, she can't keep her love to herself!

Have you seen the boyfriend? (NO!)
Not only ugly no future (NO!)
Do you think we owe it to her as friends
To tell her that she is really a slut
To tell her exactly what is what
If she's not careful she won't have any friends at all

Did you see who she is dating?
He's hardly a man at all
He barely smiles and when
He talks he lisps

I'd rather go to bed with a broom
I'd rather tell the truth than lie
If friends can't tell you the truth
Then really who will

I know you'd tell me if
I was petty
I know you'd say if I was small
If your friends can't tell you
Who bloody hell will?!

She's our best friend but
She's ruining her life
She'll only make it worse if
She becomes his wife
She's not getting any younger
But can't she do better than this?

Oh she can do better
Oh she can do better
Oh she can do better than this
Oh she can do better than this

Future Farmers of America

Born on a farm in a transatlantic moonlight
Split like a cord of wood my family broke up
Sold like a piece of steer a piece of meat a cow
A breathing piece of shit

Picked for my age for my strength and makeup
Called for: I was tall I was big I could hold up
A tree or a piece of steel I could do
What my fat owner can't

Future farmers of America

I'm always watching the way his wife looks me over
I have a sex twice as big as her husband's
If I wasn't so large so strong so pale
I'd disappear under a bush

Colorless men and ladies of the world unite
Kill your master with one cut of your knife
Kill them during sex kill them during talk
Kill them whenever you can

Future farmers of America

These stupid black owners are foreigners
to affairs of heart
Look at me! I'll never own land that I
work on!
Every one of us here shares a surname
This father must die

I was born on the dark cusp of twilight
My father was dark my mother was light
Look at me I'm strong
I could crush him in my fist

I could crush him in my
I could crush him in my
I could crush him in my fist
Future farmers of America
I could crush him in my fist

Putting on a New Skin

Putting on a new skin
Covering up the old blood
Remember where we came from
Sticky black primordial mud

Looking like a rhino
Looking like a tiger
With so many colors here
Why do I like you just in black?
Why do I love you just in black?

Purple yellow green chartreuse
Silver gray don't be obtuse
Unless you're just an old recluse
I love you in black

Putting on a new skin
Looking for a good time
Getting rid of old looks
Searching for newly sublime!
Searching for newly sublime!

Cobra blue and cancer brown
Torrential white and juicy mauve
I just want to get my old skin off
'Cause I love you in black
'Cause I love you in black

Reverse Diminuendo

It must be nice to have a home
That always stays under your feet
That can always be depended on
One place to eat and sleep

How nice it must be to have a rug
On which to stretch your legs
A T-bone steak beside me
I want to be a dog

It must be nice to have a home
A place that you can trust
That stays forever in one spot
And never moves about

It must be nice to have a fire lit
And stretch out on a rug
A meaty bone next to your nose
I want to be a dog

I want to be a dog
I want to be a dog
With a T-bone in my paws
I want to be a dog

Turning Time Around

(Priscilla)
What do you call love
(Nick)
Well, I call it Harry
(Priscilla)
Please I'm being serious
What do you call love

(Nick)
Well I don't call it family
And I don't call it lust
And as we all know—marriage isn't a must
And I suppose in the end it's a matter of trust
If I had to—I'd call love time

(Priscilla)
What do you call love
Can't you be more specific
What do you call love
Is it more than the heart's hieroglyphic

(Nick)
Time has no meaning
No future no past
And when you're in love
You don't have to ask
There's never enough time
To hold love in your grasp
Turning time around

(Both)
Turning time around
That is what love is
Turning time around
Yes, that is what love is
(Nick)
My time is your time
When you're in love
(Priscilla)
And time is what you never have enough of
(Nick)
You can't see or hold it
It's exactly like love

(Both)
Turning time around
Turning time around
Turning time around

Into the Divine

I think you're so beautiful
I think you're so kind
And I think I would miss you
If you disappear into the divine

I think of an apple core
When you start thinking of god
And I know I would miss you
If you disappear into the divine

I think you're so beautiful
As beautiful as the blackened space and stars
But all I see is a coreless seed
When you cry for a god who's not there

But I think you're so beautiful
And I see you as a sun
That shines out through these galaxies
Shimmering and warm

And I think you're so beautiful
And if there's one thing I believe at all
It's how much I would miss you
If you disappeared into the divine
It's how much I would miss you
If you disappeared into the divine

Why Do You Talk

Why do you talk
Why do you waste time
Saying the same old thing
It should be a crime

You never listen
Instead you stammer
As though you're interesting
And full of glamour
As though you're interesting
And full of glamour

Why do you talk so much
Why don't you shut up
You have nothing to say
You lack drama

It's the same old thing
You'd like to know why
Who made the earth move
Who made the sky high
Who made the earth move
Who made the sky high
Who made your blood red
Who made you think thoughts
Who made you breathe a
breath
Tell me, why do you talk
Tell me, why do you talk
Tell me, why do you talk
Tell me, why do you talk

Why do you always talk
Why do you make sounds
Why don't you listen
Why do you talk so much
Why don't you listen
Why do you talk so much

Why don't you shut up

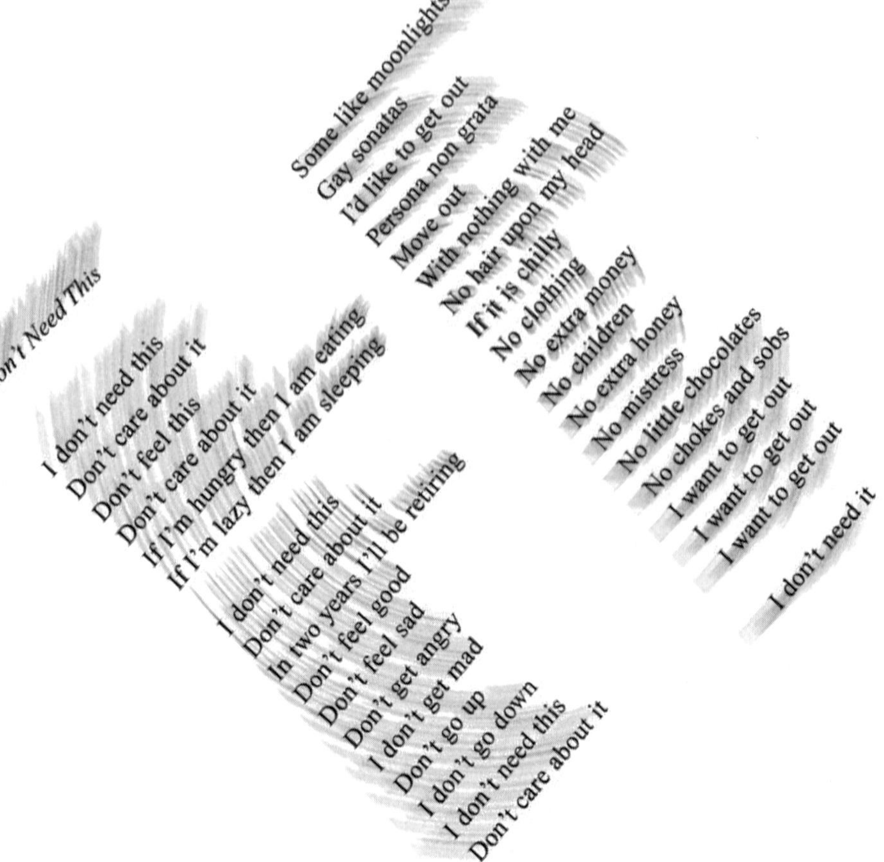
on't Need This
I don't need this
Don't care about it
Don't feel this
Don't care about it
If I'm hungry then I am eating
If I'm lazy then I am sleeping
I don't need this
Don't care about it
In two years I'll be retiring
Don't feel good
Don't feel sad
Don't get angry
I don't get mad
Don't go up
I don't go down
I don't need this
Don't care about it
Some like moonlights
Gay sonatas
I'd like to get out
Persona non grata
Move out
With nothing with me
No hair upon my head
If it is chilly
No clothing
No extra money
No children
No extra honey
No mistress
No little chocolates
No chokes and sobs
I want to get out
I want to get out
I want to get out
I don't need it

Talking Book

I wish I had a talking book
That told me how to act and look
A talking book that contained keys
To past and present memories

A talking book that said your name
So if you were gone you'd still remain
More than a picture on a shelf
In imagination I could touch
A talking, talking book

I wish I had a talking book
Filled with buttons you could push
Containing looks and sights
Your touch
Your look your eyes your scent
Your touch
Your feel your breath
Your sounds your sighs
How much I'd live to ask it why
One must live and one must die

I wish I had a talking book
By my side so I could look
And touch and feel and dream a look
Much bigger than a talking book
A taste of lovings future and past
Is that so much to really ask
In this one moment's time in space
Can our love really be replaced
By a talking book?

On the Run

You don't ever compromise
I see the pain in your eyes
Don't you worry, the game is won
I'll be there on the run

I'll make you happy, the others are thick
Just call me up, I'll be your big stick
They do it for money that's what they call fun
I'll be there on the run

A room with thirteen chairs
Three lions, ten polar bears
An ice cube the size of the sun
I'll be there on the run

I see pain in your eyes
And you know I sympathize
I'll come runnin' the game is won
I'll be there on the run

We have never compromised
I'll say I love you a million times
Don't you forget it the game is won
I'll be there on the run

Don't you forget it, the game is won
I'll be there on the run

ECSTASY

Ecstasy

They call you Ecstasy
Nothing ever sticks to you
Not Velcro not Scotch Tape
Not my arms dipped in glue
Not if I wrap myself in nylon
A piece of duct tape down my back
Love pierced the arrow with the 12
And I can't get you back
Ecstasy, Ecstasy
Ecstasy

Across the streets an old Ford
They took off its wheels
The engine is gone
In its seat sits a box
With a note that says, "Goodbye Charlie - thanks a lot"
I see a child through a window with a bib
And I think of us and what we almost did
The Hudson rocketing with light
The ships pass the Statue of Liberty at night
They call it Ecstasy. Ecstasy
Ecstasy. Ecstasy

Some men call me St. Ivory
Some call me St. Maurice
I'm smooth as alabaster
With white veins running through my cheeks
A big stud through my eyebrow
A scar on my arm that says "Domain"
I put it over the tattoo
That contained your name
They called you Ecstasy Ecstasy Ecstasy
They call you Ecstasy Ecstasy Ecstasy

The moon passing through a cloud
A body facing up is floating towards a crowd
And I think of a time and what I couldn't do
I couldn't hold you close, I couldn't I couldn't become you

They call you Ecstasy
I can't hold you down I can't hold you up
I feel like that car that I saw today
No radio no engine no hood
I'm going to the café I hope they've got music
And I hope that they can play
But if we have to part I'll have a new scar right over my heart——I'll call it Ecstasy
Ecstasy Ecstasy Ecstasy
Ecstasy Ecstasy Ecstasy

Mystic Child

It was only the time of the newly born dead
With the wispy cobwebs in your head
The polar moon looked out instead
Going wild

Liquor shifting through the brain
The manic-depressive goes insane
Going wild going wild

Desperate anger hits the streets
By the foul smelling river by the meat market
Going wild mystic child

In the winter with the frozen toes
Looking out the big windows
To fly
Going wild

Situation X out of control
My eyes half opened like a mole
Who smiles
Going wild

In the mystic morning where the river meets
The hurdy-gurdy of the hip hop beat
5 A.M. the viscous street
Wild goin' wild

Out the window like a flash
Falling through a rooftop crash
Blind
Goin' wild

Sick and misty like a pup by the curb he's
Throwin' up
Wild
Like a child

If he can't have all that relates
To testify that he is great
He'll cut someone with a broken plate
And stand upon the subway grate
And smile
Goin' wild goin' wild with a smile

Holy morning
Sun is up and someone
Here has lost his cups
The dawn is tattered all cut up
Goin' wild like a mystic child
Like a mystic child

Sunday morning looking down from the rooftop
Goin' wild
With a smile- mystic child

Top of the world he's got it made
His rings are gold his braids are jade
He jumped to the street-he's got it made
Goodbye child
Goodbye child
Mystic child
Goin' wild

Paranoia Key of E

How come you say you will and then you won't
You change your mind and then you say you don't
The mystery is why I play the goat
The mystery you call love

Sometimes you're like an eagle strong like a rock
Other times it seems you get unlocked
And all of your worst fears come tumbling out
Into the street into the snow

I remember when you had a dream
Everything was what it seemed to be
But now nightmares replace everything
And everything you see is wrong

You said we'd meet but you're 2 hours late
You said you thought someone had picked your gate
So you hid and were afraid to wait
Seeing shadows in the snow

Now your friend Godfrey is a perfect choice
One minute down next time rejoice
He seems to have found the perfect voice
Paranoia key of E

Let's say everything he says is true
You love me but I cheat on you
And in my bedroom is a female zoo
Worse than Clinton in prime time
I swear to you I'm not with Jill or Joyce
Or Cyd or Sherry or Darlene or worse
I'm not kissing you while inside I curse
Paranoia key of E

Let's play a game the next time we meet
I'll be the hands and you be the feet
And together we will keep the beat
To paranoia key of E

Now you know mania's in the key of B
Psychosis in the key of C
Let's hope that we're not meant to be
In paranoia key of E

Anorexia is in G flat
And F is anything I've left out
Dyslexia, Kleptomania and Vertigo
Patricide A, matricide D the same schizos
Paranoia key of E

Let's have a coda in the key of K
Something that only we can play
Maybe we'll light up like a 100 K
Paranoia out of Key
Paranoia key of E

Mad

Mad- you just make me mad
I hate your silent breathing in the night
Sad- you make me sad
When I juxtapose your features I get sad

I know I shouldn't a had someone else in our bed
But I was so tired I was so tired
Who would think you'd find a bobby pin
It just makes me mad
Makes me mad
It just makes me, makes me mad

Glad-when I'm gone your glad
That overwhelming tension dissipates
Tad- you think I'm a baby
Nobody likes to hear "why don't you grow up"
At dawn

I know I shouldn't a had someone else in our bed
But I was so tired, so tired
Who would think you'd find a bobby pin
It makes me mad
Makes me mad
Don't you know it just makes me mad

Dumb - you're dumb as my thumb
In the wistful morning you throw a coffee cup at my head
Scum - you said I'm scum
What a very lovely feminine thing to do

Bark - why don't you just bark
Sit, come, stay, are the perfect words meant for you
Ass - you says I'm an ass
You better call 911 'cause I'm gonna hold you tight

I know I shouldn't a had someone else in our bed
But I was so tired so tired
You said you're out of town for the night
And I believed in you
I believed you
And I was so tired
It makes me so mad
It makes me so mad
Dumb...

Modern Dance

Maybe I should go and live in Amsterdam
in a side street near a big canal
spend my evenings in the van Gogh Museum
what a dream van Gogh Museum

or maybe it's time to see Tangiers
a different lifestyle some different fears
and maybe I should be in Edinburgh
in a kilt in Edinburgh

Doin' a modern dance
Doin' a modern dance

Or maybe I should get a farm in southern France
Where the winds are wispy
And the villagers dance
And you and I we'd sleep beneath a moon
Moon in June and sleep till noon

And maybe you and I could fall in love
Regain the spirit that we once had
You'd let me hold you and touch the night
That shines so bright
So bright with fright

Doin' a modern dance
Doin' a modern dance

Shit maybe I could go to Yucatan
where women are women a man's a man
no one confused
ever loses place
with their place
in the human race

Maybe I'm not cut out for city life
the smell of exhaust the smell of strife
and maybe you don't want to be a wife
it's not a life being a wife

Doin' a modern dance
Doin' a modern dance

So maybe I should go to Tanganyika
Where the rivers run
down mountains tall and steep
Or go to India to study chants
And lose romance to a mantra's dance

I need a guru I need some law
Explain to me the things we saw
And why it always comes to this
It's all downhill after the first kiss

Maybe... I should move to Rotterdam
Maybe... move to Amsterdam
I should move to Ireland
Italy, Spain, Afghanistan
Where there is no rain

Or maybe I should just learn a modern dance
Where roles are shifting the modern dance
You never touch you don't know who you're with
This week this month this time of year
This week this month this time of year

Doin' a Modern Dance
You don't know who you're with-modern dance
I should move to Pakistan go to Afghanistan- dance
You don't know who you're with- dance
You don't know who you're with-modern dance
And maybe you don't want to be a wife
It's not a life being a wife
Doin' a modern dance
You never touch you don't know who you're with
Dance-modern dance
The roles are shifting - dance

Tatters

Some couples live in harmony
Some do not
Some couples yell and scream
Some do not
But what you said was something that I can't forget
It echoes in my head like a bullet made of lead

Some people yell and scream and some do not
Some people sacrifice their lives and some do not
Some people wait for sleep to take them away
While others read books endlessly
Hoping problems will go away

I know you're hoping everything works out
Neither one of us is the type who shouts
You sleep in the bedroom
While I pace up and down the hall
Our baby stares at both of us
Wondering which one of us to call

I guess it's true that not every match burns bright
I guess it's true not all that I say is right
But what you said still bounces around in my head
Who thought this could happen to us
When we first went to bed

I'm told in the end that none of this matters
All couples have troubles and none of this matters
But what you said still echoes in my head
And I'm still in the hallway downstairs sleeping alone
instead

I know you don't care but here's my last thought
Not that it matters, but here's the last thing I thought
Our little thing is lying here in tatters
And you my dear don't have any manners

Sad to leave this way - to leave it all in tatters
Saddening to leave this way - to leave it all in tatters
I suppose we all could say that nothing of it matters
But still it's sad to see everything in tatters

Baton Rouge

When I think of you Baton Rouge
I think of a mariachi band
I think of 16 and a crisp green football field
I think of the girl I never had

When I think of you Baton Rouge
I think of a back seat in a car
The windows are foggy
And so are we
As the police asked for our I.D.

So helpless
So helpless
Ooohhh so helpless
Ooohhh so helpless
Ooohhh so helpless
So helpless

Well I once had a car
Lost it in a divorce
The judge was a woman of course
She said give her the car and the house and your taste
Or else I set the trial date

So now when I think of you Baton Rouge
And the deep southern belles with their touch
I wonder where love ends and hate starts to blush
In the fields in the swamps in the rush

In the terra-cotta cobwebs of your mind
When did you start seeing me
As a spider spinning web
Of malicious intent
And you as poor poor me
At the fire at the joint
This disinterred and broken mount
In the bedroom in the house
Where we were unmarried

So helpless
So helpless
So helpless

When was I the villain in your heart
Putting the brake on your start
You slapped my face and cried and screamed
That's what marriage came to mean
The bitterest ending of a dream

You wanted children
And I did not
Was that what it was all about
You might get a laugh when you hear me shout
You might get a laugh when you hear me shout
I wish I had
So helpless
So helpless
So helpless
So helpless
So helpless
So helpless

Sometimes when I think of Baton Rouge
I see us with 2 1/2 strapping sons
1 1/2 flushed daughters preparing to marry
And two fat grandsons I can barely carry

Daddy, uncle, family gathered there for grace
A dog in a barbecue pit goes up in space
The dream recedes in the morning with a bad aftertaste
And I'm back in the big city worn from the race of the
chase what a waste

So thanks for the card
The announcement of child
And I must say you and Sam look great
Your daughter's gleaming in that white wedding dress
with pride
Sad to say I could never bring that to you
That wide smile
So I try not to think of Baton Rouge
Or of a mariachi band
Or of 16 and a crisp green football field
And the girl I never had

So helpless
So helpless
So helpless

The White Prism

There's a white prism with phony jism
Spread across its face
And the soulful convicts forever interred
Lose the smile across their faces
The smile that registered hopes or dreams
Has proven just a waste
And I'm the indentured servant
Forever in his place

I wish I built a cabinet of shiny bolts and wood
Secret draws and hiding places sculpted out of wood
Secret places secret lies in a desk lying alone
A secret letter written to you
To be read when you're alone

It says:
I'm your indentured servant
I can no longer pretend
That I'm a lover or an equal
I'm not even a friend
I'm not good enough to serve you
I'm not good enough to stay
So it is that I beseech you
To please turn me away

I'm asking you to let me go
It hurts me when you're sad
And I can not do better than this
Which must surely make you mad
I'd be better off in your cabinet or in a prison made of cloth
Crouched beneath your dress I come
Shooting little spurts

I'm your indentured servant
But even I have pride
In what I make or say or do
Although I've lots to hide
I hide from freedom and I hide from you
'cause you've found me out
I belong in prison beneath your legs
In a cabinet that I've built
Beneath a candle in a secret drawer in a prison by a moat

I'm your indentured servant
And I'm asking you to leave
Me outside this prison cell where only you can breathe

I'm your indentured servant but I'm asking you for this
Please release me from this love and do it with a kiss
I'm your indentured servant
I'm the one you'll miss
Do it with a kiss
Do it with a kiss
Do it with a kiss
I'm the one you'll miss

Big Sky

Big sky holding up the sun
Big sky holding up the moon
Big sky holding down the sea
But it can't hold us down anymore

Big sky holding up the stars
Big sky holding Venus and Mars
Big sky catch you in a jar
But it can't hold us down anymore

Big sky big enormous place
Big wind blow all over the place
Big storm wrecking havoc and waste
But it can't hold us down anymore

Big goals big ambitious goals
Big talk- talking till I fold
Big wind- talking through torrential love
But it can't hold us down anymore

Big sin big original sin
Paradise where I've never been
Big snake break the skin
But you can't hold us down anymore

A big house holds a family
A big room it holds you and me
It's a big mess and baby makes three
But you can't hold us down anymore

Big news they're out of their heads
Big big big news let's fuck them instead
There's a big joke did they think we were monks
But they can't hold us down anymore

A big doll big enormous eyes
Big love holds you in a vise
A big man who cut them down to size
They can't hold us down anymore

The Rock Minuet

Paralyzed by hatred and a piss ugly soul
If he murdered his father he thought he'd become whole
While listening at night to an old radio
Where they danced to the rock minuet

In the gay bars in the back of the bar
He consummated hatred on a cold sawdust floor
While the jukebox played backbeats
He sniffed coke off a jar
While they danced to a rock minuet

School was a waste he was meant for the street
But school was the only way the army could be beat
The two whores sucked his nipples 'til he came on their feet
As they danced to the rock minuet

He dreamt that his father was sunk to his knees
His leather belt tied so tight that it was hard to breathe
And the studs from his jacket were as cold as a breeze
As he danced to a rock minuet

He pictured the bedroom where he heard the first cry
His mother on all fours with his father behind
And her yell hurt so much he had wished he'd gone blind
And rocked to a rock minuet

In the back of the warehouse were a couple of guys
They had tied someone up and sewn up their eyes
And he got so excited he came on his thighs
When they danced to the rock minuet

On Ave. B someone cruised him one night
He took him in an alley and then pulled a knife
And thought of his father as he cut his windpipe
And finally danced to the rock minuet

In the curse of the alley the thrill of the street
On the bitter cold docks
Where the outlaws all meet
In euphoria drug in euphoria heat
You could dance to the rock minuet
In the thrill of the needle and anonymous sex
You could dance to the rock minuet

So when you dance hard - slow dancing
When you dance hard - slow dancing
When you dance hard - slow dancing
When you dance to the rock minuet

Like a Possum

Good morning it's Possum Day
Feel like a possum in every way – like a possum
Possum whiskers, possum face
Possum breath and a possum taste
Like a possum

Possum tales possum eyes
Possum bones possum thighs
Like a possum
Possum shots possum runs
Possum sleeps to possum drums
Calm as an angel

Good morning it's Possum Day
I feel like a possum in every way
Like a possum
Wake up with a possum smile
Look at me! Look at this smile
Like a possum

Things are all right don't worry about this
My mind's amiss I've lost the kiss
My smile is leaden my gait is rubber
And I say as one possum to another
Like a possum
Calm as an angel

The only thing I hope to never see
Is another possum in this tree
Playing possum
Just like a possum

I got a hole in my heart the size of a truck
It won't be filled by a one-night fuck
Slurping and squeezing ain't it just my luck
Got a hole in my heart the size of a truck
The size of a truck

The devil tried to fill me up but my down was high
As the sky is up
Ain't that just my luck
Calm as an angel

Smoking crack with a downtown flirt
Shooting and coming 'til it hurts
Calm as an angel

They're mating like apes in the zoo
One for me and one for you
Wouldn't it just be lovely

Another useless night in bed
By the Hudson River
The rollerbladers giving head
Used condoms float on the river edge's head
Wouldn't it be lovely
Wouldn't it be lovely

I got a hole in my heart the size of a truck
It won't be filled by one night fuck
Like a possum
Like a possum
Calm as an angel

You know me I like to dance a lot
With different selves who cancel out one another
I'm the only one left standing

One likes muscles, oil, and dirt
And the other likes the women with the butt that hurts
Like a possum

The devil tried to fill me up
But my down was high as the sky is up
Calm as an angel

I got a hole in my heart the size of a truck
And it won't be filled by a one-night fuck
Like a Possum

You know me I like to drink a lot
And carry on-don't know which self will show up
Over the 5 A.M. sun, the moon is shining
Over the docks shining
Calm as an angel

Girls in the market know what I'm about
They pinch their nipples and they lift their skirts
With a pierced tongue licking below a stained tee shirt

Look at this smile
My mind's amiss

Smoking crack with a downtown flirt
Shooting and coming 'til it hurts
Calm Calm
Sitting on a curb I throw a rock
At the passing meat market trucks
It's just my luck
I'm the only one left standing

Now you know me I like to drink a lot
The only one left standing
The girls in the market know what I'm about
They pinch their nipples and they lift their skirts
Licking below a stained tee shirt
Calm as an angel

Smoking crack with a downtown flirt
Shooting and coming baby 'til it hurts
Wouldn't it be,
Wouldn't it be,
Wouldn't it be love
Wouldn't it be lovely
Calm as an angel

Got a hole in my heart the size of a truck
It won't be filled by a one-night fuck
Ain't it just my luck
Got a hole in my heart the size of a truck

Another useless night in bed
Walk down to the Hudson River getting head
Calm calm calm calm as an angel
Don't know why baby I'm still here
Strong and fearless in the outside air
I'm the only one left standing

I'm the only one, the only one
The only one left standing
I'm the only one
I'm the only one left standing
Calm as an angel
I'm the only one
I'm the only one
The only one left standing
Calm as an angel

Shooting an coming 'til it hurts
O'holy morning
Calm as an angel

The Velvet Underground & Nico (Verve, 1967)

Sunday Morning**

Black Angel's Death Song**

All Songs Published by Oakfield Avenue Music Ltd.
*All rights administered by Screen Gems–EMI Music Inc. (BMI) except **Published by John Cale Music, Inc. (BMI) / Oakfield Avenue Music, Ltd. All rights administered by Screen Gems–EMI Music Inc. (BMI)*

White Light/White Heat (Verve, 1967)

The Gift**

Here She Comes Now**

Sister Ray**

All Songs Published by Oakfield Avenue Music Ltd.
*All rights administered by Screen Gems–EMI Music Inc. (BMI) except **Published by John Cale Music, Inc. (BMI) / Oakfield Avenue Music, Ltd. All rights administered by Screen Gems–EMI Music Inc. (BMI)*

The Velvet Underground (MGM, 1969)

All Songs Published by Oakfield Avenue Music Ltd.
All rights administered by Screen Gems–EMI Music Inc. (BMI)

1969 Velvet Underground Live

Sweet Jane (Prototype)

New Age (Prototype)

Over You

Published by Oakfield Avenue Music Ltd.
All rights administered by Screen Gems–EMI Music Inc. (BMI)

Loaded (Cotillian, 1970)

Published by Oakfield Avenue Music Ltd.
All rights administered by Screen Gems–EMI Music Inc. (BMI)

VU

Stephanie Says

Temptation Inside Your Heart***

One of These Days***

I'm Sticking with You***

Published by Oakfield Avenue Music Ltd.
All rights administered by Screen Gems–EMI Music Inc. (BMI)
****Published by John Cale Music, Inc. (BMI)*

Another View (Polygram, 1986)

Hey Mr. Rain**

Ferryboat Bill**

***Published by John Cale Music, Inc. (BMI) / Oakfield Avenue Music Ltd.*
All rights administered by Screen Gems–EMI Music Inc. (BMI)

The Velvet Underground Live MCMXCIII

Velvet Nursery Rhyme**

Coyote**

***Published by John Cale Music, Inc. (BMI) /Metal Machine Music, Inc.*
All rights administered by Screen Gems–EMI Music, Inc. (BMI)

Nico: Chelsea Girl (Polygram, 1967)

Wrap Your Troubles in Dreams

*Chelsea Girls ***

Published by Oakfield Avenue Music Ltd.
All rights administered by Screen Gems–EMI Music, Inc. (BMI)
***Published by John Cale Music, Inc. (BMI) / Oakfield Avenue Music Ltd.*
All rights administered by Screen Gems–EMI Music Inc. (BMI)

Lou Reed (RCA, 1972)

Published by Oakfield Avenue Music Ltd.
All rights administered by Screen Gems–EMI Music, Inc. (BMI)

Transformer (RCA, 1972)

Published by Oakfield Avenue Music Ltd.
All rights administered by Screen Gems–EMI Music, Inc. (BMI)

Berlin (RCA, 1973)

Published by Oakfield Avenue Music Ltd.
All rights administered by Screen Gems–EMI Music, Inc. (BMI)

Sally Can't Dance (RCA, 1974)

Published by Oakfield Avenue Music Ltd.
All rights administered by Screen Gems–EMI Music, Inc. (BMI)

Metal Machine Music (RCA, 1975)
Liner Notes by Lou Reed

Coney Island Baby (RCA, 1975)

Published by Oakfield Avenue Music Ltd.
All rights administered by Screen Gems–EMI, Inc. (BMI)

Rock and Roll Heart (Arista, 1976)

Published by Metal Machine Music, Inc.
All rights administered by Screen Gems–EMI, Inc. (BMI)

Street Hassle (Arista, 1978)

Published by Metal Machine Music, Inc.
All rights administered by Screen Gems–EMI, Inc. (BMI)

The Bells (Arista, 1979)

Published by Metal Machine Music, Inc.
All rights administered by Screen Gems–EMI, Inc. (BMI)

Growing Up in Public (Arista, 1980)

Published by Metal Machine Music, Inc.
All rights administered by Screen Gems–EMI, Inc. (BMI)

The Blue Mask (RCA, 1982)

Published by Metal Machine Music, Inc.
All rights administered by Screen Gems–EMI, Inc. (BMI)

Legendary Hearts (RCA, 1983)

Published by Metal Machine Music, Inc.
All rights administered by Screen Gems–EMI, Inc. (BMI)

New Sensations (RCA 1984)

Published by Metal Machine Music, Inc.
All rights administered by Screen Gems–EMI, Inc. (BMI)

Mistrial (RCA, 1986)

Published by Metal Machine Music, Inc.
All rights administered by Screen Gems–EMI, Inc. (BMI)

New York (Sire, 1989)

Published by Metal Machine Music, Inc.
All rights administered by Screen Gems–EMI, Inc. (BMI)

Songs for Drella (Sire, 1990)

Published by John Cale Music, Inc. (BMI) / Metal Machine Music, Inc.
All rights administered by Screen Gems–EMI, Inc. (BMI)

Magic and Loss (Sire, 1992)

Published by Metal Machine Music, Inc.
All rights administered by Screen Gems–EMI, Inc. (BMI)

Set the Twilight Reeling (Warner Bros., 1996)

Published by Lou Reed Music.
All rights administered by EMI Blackwood Music, Inc. (BMI)

Time Rocker (1996)

Published by Lou Reed Music.
All rights administered by EMI Blackwood Music, Inc. (BMI)

Miscellaneous

Ocean

Oakfield Avenue Music Ltd. (BMI) administered by Screen Gems-EMI Music, Inc. (Velvet Underground Peel Slowly and See, Box Set, Polygram, 1995)

You Can Dance

Such a Pretty Face

Affirmative Action (PO #99)

Better Get Up and Dance

Unpublished

Here Comes the Bride

John Cale Music, Inc.(BMI) / Oakfield Avenue Music Ltd. (BMI) administered by Screen Gems-EMI Music, Inc.
(Velvet Underground Peel Slowly and See, Box Set, Polygram, 1995)

My Name Is Mok

Rock and Rule (MGM/UA, 1984)

One World One Voice

Why Can't I Be Good*

**Faraway So Close! (EMI/Electrola, 1993)*

You'll Know You Were Loved

Friends (Reprise, 1995)

Is Anybody Listening

The Original Motion Picture Soundtrack, Mad City *(Warner Bros., 1996)*

Little Sister

The Original Motion Picture Soundtrack, Get Crazy *(Morocco/Motown, 1983)*

Letters to the Vatican

Nothing But the Truth (Electra, 1988)

The Calm Before the Storm

Nothing But the Truth (Electra, 1988)

Something Happened

The Original Motion Picture Soundtrack, Permanent Record *(Epic/CBS Records, 1988)*

Downtown Dirt (Prototype)

Published by Metal Machine Music, Inc. administered by Screen Gems—EMI, Inc. (BMI) (Between Thought and Expression The Lou Reed Anthology BMG 1992)